Still Standing

FROM THE SHORES OF BELFAST TO THE LIGHTS OF DUBLIN

DENISE ROBINSON

Copyright © 2022 by Denise Robinson
All rights reserved.
Some names and identifying details have been changed to protect the privacy of the people involved.

This book is dedicated to the memory of my dad,
William J. Robinson MBE

I miss you. Your courage, determination, loyalty, selflessness,
and modesty remain a source of inspiration to me.
Thank you for being you.

Contents

Preface	1
Prologue	3
The Move	4
Home	8
Growing Up	13
Independence	18
First Love	22
A New Love	32
The Big Day	37
Heaven	41
Freedom	47
Obsession	51
Whirlwind	55
Interlude	61
Daredevil	63
Dublin	71

Colorado	74
Spring	78
Summer	80
Happiness	82
Honeymoon	90
Lovebug	95
A Day at the Palace	99
Descent	102
Christmas	108
Cape Town	111
Safari	117
Surfacing	119
Rebirth	124
Rome	131
Nights in Marbella	134
From Cyprus to Los Angeles	140
What Happens in Vegas	146

The Captain	150
On A Wing and A Prayer	157
The Next Big Love	162
Options	170
Holding Pattern	174
Breaking Point	179
The Beginning of The End	182
Dark Days	192
The Bright Side	199
Aftermath	202
A New Leaf	208
Debut	213
Snowed In	216
Going Out	222
Giving Back	228
Déjà Vu	234
Apocalypse	238

Reopening	245
The New Normal	267
P.S.	273
Acknowledgments	277

Preface

I have led a colorful and wonderful life, which has been made richer by the pain and heartbreak I have experienced. I have loved and lost many times over, and through this process I have learned so much about myself. I am sharing my story in the hope that it will help anyone who finds themselves struggling to move forward after enduring any kind of loss.

Life is filled with new beginnings. No matter your age or your past experiences, you can gain the inner strength to start anew. You can find the self-love to heal yourself from a broken heart. And you can achieve the peace and positivity that will allow you to open yourself up to love again.

I hope that my story will inspire you to move past heartbreak or loss, to start loving yourself again, and to embark upon your next adventure.

—Denise Robinson

Dún Laoghaire, June 2022

Prologue

I've never been a fan of the rain. But the wind is a force of nature to which I can relate. On this bright, breezy Dún Laoghaire morning in 2018, in my new home by the sea, it was pushing me in the right direction. A year earlier, I had been here to visit my friend Richard, who lived only a short train journey from the bustling city center. As I admired his lovely home with its beautiful views, I had no way of knowing that I would soon make South Dublin my home. I could never have guessed I would be standing here a year later, on my forty-ninth birthday, bursting with joy. How had I gotten here?

I was a Northern Ireland girl from a good family. My father had adored me. My relationship with my mother had been fraught. In fairness, she had done her best. Aren't we all victims of our parents' parenting? It was tough, and I grew up looking over my shoulder. For years, I had wandered down the wrong path. Several dubious turns had carried me through two failed marriages and an unfulfilling long-term relationship. I had tolerated shoddy behavior and probably stayed too long. Men have a way of getting between me and my dreams.

Realizing I had lost my way was only half the battle. The other half was taking those first tentative steps out of my comfort zone. I managed to offload all my designer clothes and fancy furniture. I no longer felt defined by them. I pulled together enough to cover the first month's rent and the deposit on a bijou apartment minutes from the pier.

Although I hadn't emerged unscathed, I had found my way out. Here I was, in Dún Laoghaire, standing on the shore of a new life. The sun was shining. The future was bright. I had a spring in my step. Life was full of possibilities. I was ready.

The Move

A week before I was due to move, I looked at my black cocker spaniel, Zara, and said, "Gosh, how will I physically get all my possessions to Dublin?"

Zara gazed back at me with her large, loving eyes and lay down, as if to say: *How would I know?*

The next day, I received a Facebook message from Gary. He had rented space from my ex-husband's family business, but I didn't really know him. Gary insisted on bringing his van and enlisting the help of a colleague to help me with the move.

He said, "Denise, I don't want money. You need help, and I'm here to help."

It was like God had sent me an angel.

At eight in the morning, we pulled up in front of my new apartment, which faces a beautiful park that comes to life every Sunday with a farmers' market. I was met by my landlord, who was touching on a hundred! Though he was a grumpy old man, he was a retired vet and loved animals, so he was fine with me having Zara in the apartment.

My friend Dave came over to help. For the last six months, I had been regularly driving back and forth between Belfast and Dublin, networking at Dublin Chamber, and attending as many events as I possibly could. In that time, I had connected with many new people, including Dave. I introduced him to Gary and his colleague, and the four of us started to unload my belongings. Everything I had brought over fitted perfectly into my new apartment. Even the curtains were perfect. It was like magic.

The apartment was in the basement of a Georgian house that contained seven other apartments. While it had seen better days, it had loads of character and reminded me of the house I had left behind. It had a beautiful walled garden for Zara to run around in, and an open fire, which were two of the most important things for me. In my previous life, I had been accustomed to more luxurious surroundings, but this was home now. I immediately felt happy and cozy.

That evening, as Dave and I were having some drinks to celebrate my arrival, my neighbor Susan popped in to introduce herself. Susan is an ex-diplomat. She's very articulate, and a real colleen, with curly black hair and pale skin. *This is great*, I thought. *Susan is single. We might become friends.*

"I'm so happy I could pinch myself," I told Dave. "The world is now my oyster. I'm in Dublin, the capital of Ireland! Just wait till you see the amazing things that are going to happen to me."

That night, Zara and I snuggled in my bed while Dave slept on the extra-large sofa that had been part of my life for a decade and a half. In the morning, I awoke to the aroma of food cooking in the People's Park. It was my first Sunday in Dún Laoghaire, and my heart was brimming with happiness and excitement. Zara, Dave, and I went out for breakfast before we started unpacking all my boxes. It was simply a great first day, walking around the park and the pier and taking in the buzz and the atmosphere.

All around us were buskers singing, people arriving on bikes after a long cycle, and families with kids and dogs. It was a bustling, happy place to be.

After Dave left that evening, I looked around at my new surroundings and felt a little flutter of nerves. The following day I would be starting a new job in this new city. And for the first time in just over a decade, I would have to answer to someone else. It wasn't even the job I really wanted. I had spent my life in print, and for the last eleven years I had run my own print broker business, which was very successful for most of those years. Print was all I knew. And, of course, selling. The December before I moved, I was offered this position at a small digital printing company. Despite my reservations, I had accepted it. I told myself it would get me into Dublin, at least. I could always find the right role after I felt settled.

Two months passed, and I could see that this job was not a good fit for me. This was a small, family-run business where everyone was stuck in their ways, and they tried to micromanage me. This did not sit well with me. I felt so homesick. I began to question whether I had done the right thing in coming here.

One night, crying, I phoned a friend from back home.

"What have I done?" I asked her.

She said, "You are so brave. It's a big step. Just give it some time."

In the morning, I got up and felt a little better.

Life has a great sense of humor and timing. It sends the right things our way at the right time. Just as I was trying to figure out what my next move would be, a friend informed me that a company she worked with in Dublin was seeking someone in sales to look after all of Ireland. This company manufactures to the pharmaceutical industry. She said they wanted someone from Northern Ireland who was living in Dublin, as they felt that people from the north were much more direct. I found this funny, but I knew what they meant. Perhaps living through the Troubles has made us harder. I had an interview, after which I was offered the job. I decided to have a few weeks off, as it was early summer. I wanted to spend some time enjoying my life by the sea. I also knew I needed to take some time to work on myself.

It requires a fair amount of confidence to sell to large multinationals, and all the rejection, pain, and heartache I had endured had caused mine to drain away. I underwent hypnosis to remove any barriers of fear and self-doubt that might stand in the way of my ability to communicate effectively. It gave me the kick that I needed, so I could walk out that door every morning and shine. In August, I got set up in my new role. I had a new company car and felt ready to take on the world.

No matter how many knocks life dealt me, I have always managed to pick myself up, dust myself down, and carry on going. At times, I have felt like giving up. I have felt that there was nothing out there for me. I have asked myself: *Why have I been sent so much pain and heartache? Why don't I live in my own home with an amazing husband and our beautiful kids? Why have I traveled down this road?*

I believe that everything happens for a reason. Perhaps my purpose is to share my story and help others. For all the sad times I have experienced, I have known great happiness. I have travelled the world in First Class. I have been deeply loved and have loved deeply.

Home

My mum and dad made a good-looking couple. My mum had an hourglass figure, cracking legs, and a massive amount of blond hair. My dad, a Teddy Boy, was extremely handsome. They loved jiving and had frequented the dance halls back in the day. They were very modest and innocent and lived a very sheltered life.

After my parents married, they saved up for their first home. This was in Belfast, and they were Catholics living in a Protestant area. They had a baby girl, who they named Brenda. Her hair had a hint of red, and—much to my mum's surprise—she was small. For some bizarre reason, my mum had expected her to be an enormous baby. Two years later they had me. I weighed ten pounds at birth and had blond hair and a big, fat face.

During the Troubles, my parents lost our home due to sectarian pressure. They decided to move to Canada, and we all were granted visas, but at the last minute my mum got cold feet. She felt we'd be too far from home. My dad got a job in Ayrshire, Scotland, and we ended up moving there. Most weekends we visited Belfast, riding the ferry from Larne to Stranraer. I remember making friends with Tracey, the little girl next door.

I was four when my brother, Barry, was born. I remember going to the hospital to see him for the first time. As we grew up, Barry and I formed a great relationship and spent lots of time playing together. He was blond, and full of fun and mischief.

I was the middle child, and you know what they say about the middle child—they always get left out. It certainly felt that way. Barry, being the youngest child and the only son, could do no wrong, and the same applied to Brenda, as the eldest child. I was the rebel, always pushing the envelope by refusing to conform to my parents' expectations. From an early age, I had big ideas and dreams. I always felt I would go far in life. Even with so much going on in my interior world, I was very shy as a child. At primary school, a teacher hit me for being too shy to re-enter the classroom after visiting the restroom. I was put into a slower class because I was too scared to speak up.

When we'd been in Scotland for two years, my mum became homesick for Northern Ireland. We moved to Antrim, a new commuter town about thirty miles outside Belfast. Many people from Belfast had moved there to escape the bombs and shootings. Antrim was a great place to grow up. My friendship group consisted of a mix of boys and girls from our estate. I have many fond memories of those innocent lovely times: building tree huts, catching tadpoles, roller-skating, playing hopscotch—all the things that kids no longer seem to do. We would go across into the adjacent field—which we called Farmer's Field—and pretend a bull was chasing us. We would just keep running. I was so happy. I stayed out until all hours of the night and came home exhausted and ravenous. Especially in the summer evenings, my mum could never get me to come home. I just loved being outdoors. I wouldn't trade those years for anything in the world.

We were living in a little piece of heaven. I never experienced the devastation of the bombings and shootings those in the city of Belfast were living through at the time. When my cousins would come over from Belfast to stay with us at the weekends, they were always reluctant to return home. They stayed with us for most of the summer holidays.

The only time I really experienced the Troubles was when we went to visit our relatives. My granny and my cousins lived in predominantly Republican areas that faced onto Protestant communities, so tension and violence always surrounded them. On many evenings, asleep in the back of the car as we were leaving my granny's house, I would be abruptly awakened by soldiers with English accents ordering us to get out of the car so they could search it. They wore warpaint on their faces and were armed with large machine guns. One evening, we had to veer around a bus that was ablaze. People were hurling petrol bombs through the air. It was a war zone. I counted myself lucky to be living in Antrim, thirty miles away from this insanity.

And yet, home wasn't an entirely conflict-free zone. My parents both worked very hard, so we never wanted for much, but they struggled at times, as many young couples do. I witnessed many horrible fights between them. I observed many interactions that no child should ever have to bear witness to, especially not between their own parents, and it felt like an inexplicable, uncontrollable mess. I understand all of this now, after undergoing many years of therapy. The discord in their relationship had deep roots reaching far back into their childhoods.

My dad's dad—my granddad—had passed away at the age of forty, leaving my granny to raise six children on her own. She was a hardworking woman who rose to the challenge, and my dad, being the eldest child, stepped up and assumed the role of a father to the best of his ability, despite still being so young himself. I love and admire my granny so much. I can also see how the tough circumstances of her life made her incredibly resilient and strong. As she had to focus on survival, she expressed her love for her children by providing for them. As a result, my dad found it very difficult to openly express love and affection. He was a genuine and honest man, and he loved us all so much, but he just could not express it.

My mum's dad had spoiled her while she was growing up, and this is partly why she became a very controlling person with many insecurities. Even though my dad loved her deeply, he didn't show it in the way she would have wanted, so she was lonely and felt deprived of affection. As her frustration turned into anger, she became increasingly abusive towards him. She would often belittle my dad, and at times she became so incensed that she would try to hit him. He simply accepted her behavior, as he felt he was to blame. He felt he was letting her down by not being able to show her the love she deserved and craved.

My mother was abusive not only to my dad, but also to me and my siblings. Children can't compare their home lives to anyone else's because you never know what's going on behind closed doors, so we thought this was normal. Only much later in life did we come to understand what was really going on. My mum had physically and emotionally abused all of us. We thought it was normal that she beat us for not doing what she wanted. I remember cowering behind my wardrobe for hours on end, and even missing dinner, because she was threatening to beat me with the leather strap. As she had done it many times before, I knew it wasn't an empty threat. This was the punishment she deemed fit for my having lost her umbrella or some similar infraction. The smallest things would set her off. These patterns of controlling and abusive behavior had repercussions that lasted well into our adult lives. I believe my mum is not a bad person. She has always loved us and truly wants the best for us, but she was often unable to express this in a healthy way.

Children deal with abuse in different ways. I continued to seek her love and approval. I would buy her gifts, send her handmade cards, and clean the house, because I wanted to feel seen by her. I know she loved all these things and I know she appreciated it, but she never could tell me. As my sister was always very quiet, my mum tended to overcompensate by paying my sister a lot more attention than she paid me. This made me feel rejected and unworthy of love.

Many years later, my mum told me, "Denise, you were always the strong independent one. I never needed to worry about you."

Little did she know that her behavior towards me had made me this way. I had needed her love and attention just as much as my sister had.

Growing Up

My mother is a very strong woman and she had great ambitions for us. She always dressed us up like little dolls. Every night, we went to bed with our hair curled in rollers for school the next day. Being an extremely talented seamstress, she made our clothes, and we always looked a million dollars. At primary school I was regularly bullied. It reached the point where I didn't even want to walk home from school for fear of getting beaten up. My mother had to go to my school to speak to the head teacher.

Looking back, I can see that my mum understood what was really going on. She knew that jealousy was a factor. I remember her telling one of the girls, "If you don't like her, then just don't look at her."

I didn't understand why these girls took such a strong dislike to me. I was not confident about my appearance and didn't see myself as they did. I was a pretty girl. I had naturally blond hair with multihued streaks that I now have to pay to get. I had a great smile, big blue eyes, and boys seemed to like me. Not that I had any interest in them; I was interested only in my friends. I played with dolls until I was twelve. That would not happen in today's world.

Over the years, my personality emerged, and my confidence blossomed. By the time I left primary school, I had become the class joker and the ringleader of my gang of friends. I then attended St Malachy's High School, a newly built secondary school in Antrim. Everyone called it the Whorehouse on the Hill, because so many of the girls were pregnant at sixteen. At first, I didn't understand why their bellies appeared swollen.

At secondary school, I retreated into myself again. The other kids started bullying me, and it was so much worse than it had been in primary school. I was often threatened after school. People called me Toff, which was short for Toffee Nose, because my mum made me carry a leather briefcase to school. I hated it and wished I had the standard casual bag everyone else carried.

I was interested only in art, drawing, painting, and spending time with my friends. I hung out with Zoe, whom everyone called a nerd; Michelle, whom they called a lesbian even though she isn't; and Andrea, whom they called Jaws because she had braces on her teeth. I guess we were classed as the nerdy bunch. We had no interest in boys. The girls who were pregnant at sixteen thought they were so much better than us. I progressed through my years at the Whorehouse on the Hill and managed to keep within my own little group of friends.

We attended Mass every Sunday with my dad. Though my mum would never go with us, she decreed that we were not to miss it. We even attended the Novenas every day for the whole week when the missionaries were at our parish. When I developed a crush on a boy called Alan, who was about eight years older than me, I would attend Mass mainly in the hopes of catching glimpses of him across the church. I remember walking to Mass on a Sunday evening in my jeans, Adidas trainers, and earphones, listening to Culture Club on my Walkman and feeling safe, without a care in the world.

When I was fourteen, I became obsessed with roller-skating. All I wanted to do was skate all day long at the Rollerdrome in Antrim town. It was a skating ring with music. I went there every Saturday with my friend Maggie Rose, and we'd stay all day until the early evening. I loved it so much. I was a tomboy and was happiest in jeans and Adidas trainers. I hated wearing skirts and dresses.

One Saturday morning, I was all set to go skating when my mum barged into my room and shouted, "You're not going out of the house looking like a boy in those horrible clothes!"

She ripped off my clothes and forced me to wear a skirt and top. I started crying. I was so upset. She carried my favorite clothes out into the field, doused them in petrol and set them on fire. Through my tears, I watched them burn. I felt so violated. To a teenager, clothes are some of the only things that are really yours. That outfit had been my uniform for life—it made me feel protected, beautiful, and safe. I had always felt so good walking up the road to the Rollerdrome in my jeans and trainers, with my white leather roller boots flung over my shoulder. I had felt invincible. I had felt like Madonna.

My mother was laughing. She said, "From now on, you will dress in the lovely clothes I worked hard to buy you."

It has taken many years of therapy for me to understand this was emotional abuse. No wonder I made all the mistakes I made later in life. I was always craving love and never felt I was good enough as I was.

Looking back on it now, I feel that my mother was jealous of my free spirit and my independence. In me, she may have seen what she wanted to be. She damaged me more than I ever knew. I love my mother and I always will. I forgive her because I know she didn't know any better. Sometimes I think new parents should be given a course on how to bring up a child and how to properly nurture them. I believe that our childhoods shape us. Our relationships with our parents greatly influence the choices we make later in life.

At sixteen, I started to go to discos. At that age I lacked confidence. I was shy, and I wasn't really interested in having a boyfriend. I wanted to become a vet, but I knew my parents didn't have the means to put me through university. I wanted to work with animals, and I dreamed of living somewhere in Africa and working at a wild rescue nature reserve. I spent my Saturday nights at a typical Eighties-style disco in a country hotel called Tullyglass, in Ballymena, about 20 miles from my home.

Tullyglass had a large function room with a dance floor in the center and two bars—one at each side. My dad brought us there and Michelle's mum collected us. We were so innocent. We would have one drink and dance all night. I would usually have a Pernod and blackcurrant, or a Pimm's and lemonade. This might seem very posh for a sixteen-year-old, but I was so clueless I had asked my mum what to order. The boys would walk around, watching the girls on the dancefloor. Whenever anyone would ask me to dance with them during the slow songs. I would reply, "Come back when the fast music's on."

I didn't want them getting too close to me. I was so happy just dancing all night. I don't think I really understood how pretty I was.

One night, a few girls I didn't know started verbally abusing me in the restroom. I felt terrified and humiliated. I just kept thinking: *Why?* I still don't know, but I remember that one of their boyfriends had fancied me.

Later, I went outside to wait for my ride. My dad was coming to collect us, and he was running late. I stood there in the freezing cold. I wrapped my arms around myself and watched the other people waiting for their taxis and buying burgers from the van that was parked there every Saturday night.

I felt someone come up behind me and yank my hair. And then, I was surrounded. Pain and shock tore through me as the girls started kicking me in the stomach and trying to kick me in the face. I covered my face with my hands to try to protect it, but they kept on kicking until my knuckles bled. I have the scars to this day. My sister tried to pitch in and help me, but they started in on her. She was like a quiet mouse. It was so unfair. There were all these boys and men just standing around, watching these vicious bitches attack us. They didn't lift a finger to help us out.

When my dad drove up, the girls ran away. Horrified, my dad immediately called the police. When they arrived, I was crying uncontrollably.

"Why?" I asked. "Why would they do this to us?"

A policeman replied, "I don't know. They're just lowlifes."

I was so sad. They had destroyed my night, and the lovely clothes that my mum had given me for Christmas were all ripped and torn. For many years afterwards, I was always very nervous around women in restrooms. I never wanted to experience that ever again.

Independence

Upon graduating from secondary school, I was accepted to study fashion design at Belfast Metropolitan College. The thought of continuing my studies and having no money didn't appeal to me. At seventeen, I wanted to be independent and be able to buy myself nice things, so I told my parents I would not be going to college. I wanted a job. I looked through the classifieds. An accountancy firm called O'Kane's was seeking an accounts typist. The office was near Queens University in Belfast.

In preparation for the interview, my mum bought me a black pencil skirt and a houndstooth jacket that accentuated my tiny little waist. With my blond hair in a bun, I looked very smart. My dad drove me to the interview and waited for me outside. The partners' secretary, who was called Nuala, came down the stairs to greet me. She was lovely and had a happy, warm, engaging face. "I love your hair and your outfit," she said.

I was still quite shy, so I didn't know what to say.

She interviewed me for about ten minutes. Then she said, "I would like to offer you the job."

"Yes!" I replied straight away. "Thank you!"

Nuala informed me I would be earning £218 a month.

"That's grand," I said. In my excitement, I had forgotten to ask her about the salary. "See you on Monday!"

I skipped out of the office feeling like I had won the lottery.

Later that day, Nuala rang me to confirm the details. She said, "You just looked so beautiful I had to give you the job."

This surprised me, as I was not that confident about my looks. She hadn't even asked me about my typing speed. To be honest, I wasn't a great typist.

I managed to get myself up every morning at six to catch a lift with my dad to the train station. I would ride the early train to Belfast and walk the three miles to the office in time to start work at nine. At the end of the workday, I would walk to the station to catch the train back to Antrim. Sometimes my dad would pick me up at the station, but usually I would just walk home. It was just so exciting to be working in the Big Smoke, as I had spent most of my life in the countryside.

I loved working at O'Kane's. When I met all the junior auditors, I remember thinking: *What a big world I am in now.* The firm was like a family to me. Nuala was my second mum, and Lind and Angela were my big sisters. Being the most junior employee, I was tasked with making the tea and coffee. I had no problem with this for the first year, and then it started to annoy me.

The clients liked me. They would give me presents at Christmas, much to the annoyance of Angela, who had worked there for many years and had never received so much as a box of chocolates. I had fun working there, and I started to grow as a person and find my personality and confidence.

My boss—Wee Hugh, as he was known—wore a hairpiece. In the summer, we could see the glue running down his forehead. He smoked cigars, so the place always stank of cigars. He would shout down the stairs at Nuala, and she would reply, "Yes, Mr. O'Kane, I am on my way!"

She ran up and down the stairs of the three-story Victorian house, her heels hammering against the steps like a machine gun. Constantly running up and down those stairs kept us all fit. Mr. O'Kane would sometimes grab our asses as we walked past. In those days, no one took sexual harassment seriously. You were expected to just laugh it off.

When I had been there for two years, I knew it was time for me to move on. As much as I loved working there, I knew there would not be any room for me to grow. I needed a higher income and I wanted to develop myself, so I decided to sign up with a recruitment agency. Before long, I interviewed for a job as a receptionist and purchase ledger clerk at a printing company called Lumaset. Though its head office was in Dublin, it had one sales director in Belfast. He was called Charlie. At my interview, he didn't ask me too many questions. I had barely left their offices when I got the call from the agency to say I had the job. Perhaps I was just lucky. Charlie was a character. He was addicted to tennis, so we knew we could always find him hitting balls at the boat club after work.

By this stage I had earned my driver's license, so my dad would let me take his car to work on the days he was not using it. I missed my O'Kane family so much that I would still go over there to have my lunch. O'Kane's was in a predominantly Catholic area, so I felt comfortable there. Lumaset was based on the Donegal Road, which was a hugely loyalist area. As a Catholic, I feared being attacked on the way out of work. Once I became better acquainted with my colleagues,

I began to enjoy working there, and I enjoyed my trips to Dublin. It is such a big and exciting city.

First Love

At around the same time as I was taking these first steps into my new world and starting work at O'Kane's, I encountered my first love. My mum would always push me to go out to discos with Brenda. At that time, we both were very innocent. I was two months away from my seventeenth birthday, and Brenda was two years older than me. Neither of us had ever kissed a boy, and the notion of having sex seemed light years away. I had long, blond hair, which my mum would patiently crimp for me, even though it took forever. I thought I was just so cool. At the same time, I didn't think I was anything special, but I had started to get a lot of attention from boys. I had a tiny waist and large breasts, but I was not aware of how beautiful my figure was.

My sister was extremely keen on a particular night at a new bar in the city called Bosco's, but I was never all that interested in going out to Belfast, as I always felt it was a dangerous place. My dad worked in the city, and one evening he would be attending a late meeting there, so he offered to drive us to the bar and collect us afterwards. Feeling comfortable with this arrangement, I agreed to accompany Brenda on her night out. Off we went into the Big Smoke.

My dad worked for British Telecom as an engineer. He had witnessed a lot of sectarian conflict in his workplace, which was based in Ballysillan, a predominantly loyalist area. Through his increased involvement with the trade unions, he became increasingly passionate about helping people of both religions to work together in harmony and advocated against sectarian intimidation between Catholics and Protestants in the workplace. This was the start of the great contribution that my dad made to Northern Ireland politics and the peace process. He wanted everyone to coexist peacefully, and he hoped for the day the Troubles would end.

He had personally witnessed many terrible things. One evening while he was working, he was commanded to drive a vehicle alleged to contain a bomb into the RUC Police Station in West Belfast. Imagine the fear he must have felt as he drove that van through those gates without knowing what would happen. Fortunately, this turned out to be a hoax bomb threat.

My dad was very charismatic, with a huge, infectious laugh. People just loved him. He was kind, considerate, and accommodating—perhaps to a fault. I guess the apple doesn't fall far from the tree.

As my dad dropped us off at Bosco's, he said he would be back to pick us up at ten. "We had better not be late," I said to Brenda as we went inside and sat down.

I was a bit of a nerd back then. I ordered my usual—Pernod and blackcurrant—which would last me all night. *Gosh,* I thought, *I love this music.* I ran onto the small, flashing dancefloor and started to dance. My sister joined me. She kept saying she fancied some guy with curly black hair. I just kept dancing and pretty much ignored her. Later, when we sat down, she hissed, "Oh my God, he's coming over. Don't you dare mention that Dad is collecting us, or I will kill you."

I rolled my eyes. She always tried to act so grown up. Curly Hair approached us with a mate who was tall and geeky. I didn't really understand what Brenda saw in this short, baby-faced boy. In his baggy, pleated trousers and cropped leather jacket he looked like one of the members of Spandau Ballet. The guys both tried to include me in the conversation, but I wasn't interested. I never wanted men to get too close to me, so I always kept my distance.

When Curly Hair offered us a lift home, I chirped, "No thanks, my daddy is collecting us!"

Brenda flashed me devil eyes.

"Come on, hurry up!" I said, as we walked towards the door. "Dad will be here soon."

Of course, after all that, my dad was uncharacteristically late. Curly Hair appeared and said, "Would you like to wait in my car?"

He waved proudly in the direction of his white XR3i, which was parked nearby.

"No, we wouldn't," I replied curtly.

My sister looked at me in horror. "Yes, we would like that very much," she said without taking her eyes off me.

I said, "No, we wouldn't! Here comes Dad."

As I ran off, Curly Hair called after my sister, "Where will you be tomorrow night?"

She said, "We go to Tullyglass every Saturday night!"

When Brenda climbed into the car, she shouted at me for being a nerd. I just ignored her.

"Who is that, anyway?" I asked her.

"His name is David. He's lovely! He lives on the Shankill Road."

I was gobsmacked. The Shankill, a predominantly loyalist area, is one of the most dangerous places in Belfast. This is where the famous Shankill Road Butchers had come from. I said, "I'm going to tell Mum about this."

"He's coming to meet us tomorrow night," she said.

"Why did you tell him our plans?"

I could still hear his Belfast accent and the way his voice had sounded like an old man's. I found him a little creepy. But if my sister liked him, then that was all that mattered.

The following night, I headed out to Tullyglass with Brenda, Michelle, Maggie Rose, and Shelly, who was a few years younger than us but was great fun. Even though I had been attacked there by a group of girls the year before, I still loved the place.

As we walked in, my sister said, "Oh my God, here comes David!"

She ran over to join him on the dancefloor. David's skinny mate was there, and he kept looking at me, but I paid him no attention. I was not remotely interested. I had fun with the girls and danced to my heart's content. My sister looked so happy.

At the end of the night, when I went to get my coat, David's friend approached me. "David doesn't fancy your sister," he said. "It's you he fancies."

"Well, I'm not interested in him," I said. "He's five years older than me."

As we waited for my dad to collect us, Brenda gave David our home telephone number so they could arrange a date. I didn't tell her what David's friend had said. Brenda was on Cloud Nine, so I didn't want to hurt her.

A few nights later, the phone rang. My dad answered it. "Denise! There's a call for you."

It was David. He had called to ask me out.

"No," I said. "And I don't appreciate you doing this to my sister." I hung up.

I went to Brenda and told her what had happened. I felt she needed to know what David was doing behind her back. She was not happy, but she didn't make an issue of it.

I said, "I won't be meeting him," and she said, "OK."

When I arrived home from work one evening a few weeks later, my mum said, "That guy David called four times tonight."

"Oh? What did he want?"

"I think he wants to invite you to a party."

"He's too old for me," I said. "I'm not going." I was enjoying my new job in the city and had no interest in boys.

"OK," she said. "I think he's going to ring back."

Later that evening, he phoned again. I said I was busy. For the next two weeks, he phoned me every evening and each time I said I was busy. Eventually, he stopped phoning me.

About a week before my seventeenth birthday, he phoned me again. "Please let me take you to the Helmsman in Bangor."

This time, I accepted his invitation. The Helmsman was a fabulous disco that I really wanted to visit, but I had never been there as it was so far away.

I told my mum, "I am only going because I want to see the place."

"OK," she said. "Be careful and have fun."

By now my sister had moved on from David, as she had found someone else to fancy, so she didn't mind that I was going on a date with him.

David drove up in his fancy white XR3i, and when I opened the car door a waft of aftershave hit me. It smelled like the perfume department at Brown Thomas. We had a great night. He was very nice, and I found him far more attractive than when we had first met.

I agreed to go out with him for my birthday. I told him I was coming up to my eighteenth, but he knew I was fibbing. He picked me up in his car and presented me with my birthday presents: my first album—*The Best of George Benson*—and a pair of Pepe jeans. At the time, I didn't own a pair of jeans. Ever since my mother had burned my favorite pair of jeans, I had started to dress quite conservatively. I always wore dresses or skirts.

"You have such an amazing figure," David said. "You should have a pair of jeans."

The next time we went out, I wore them and felt very sexy.

After that, David would drive up from Belfast to collect me in his XR3i every weekend and we would go out somewhere. After our night out, we would snog in the car at Antrim Lough. It was full of cars with their windows all steamed up. One evening, David started pressuring me to have sex. I demanded that he bring me home. I was very annoyed.

When I got home, I told my mum what had happened.

She said, "Right, that's it! He is far too old for you. Tell him you don't want to see him anymore."

When he phoned me the next day, I said, "I don't want to have a boyfriend. Just leave me alone."

Sex was never discussed in our home. I have never seen my parents or my siblings naked. To this day, I am quite reserved about sex and nudity. Throughout my life, men have always viewed me as sexy, and I could never really understand why. I was not particularly confident about my appearance. Looking back now, I understand that I never loved myself for who I was.

A few months passed. A few phone calls later, I decided to go on another date with David. This is where it started: my first love, relationship, and marriage. I was seventeen and about to embark on my first sexual experience. I had no clue about how it should be and what to expect.

Although David is a handsome guy, as a child he had been involved in a car accident, and I believe this had caused him to harbor some insecurities. His obsession with me stemmed from these issues, and from his relationship with his overprotective mother, who was overprotective. She may have overcompensated because she blamed herself for his accident, and this likely contributed to David's issues. He is extremely needy, insecure, possessive, and jealous. At the time, I didn't recognize these characteristics—I thought this must be real love. Having never been shown a healthy kind of love by my mother, I didn't know what real love would look like.

While most girls my age were out at discos and meeting boys, I was dining at fancy restaurants and going to the cinema on most nights. David would shower me with lavish gifts, and I would feel obliged to capitulate to his demands. Whenever I wanted to go out with my friends, he would start an argument with me, and it made me so upset and anxious. This made it impossible to do anything on my own—it didn't feel worth fighting for.

I spent every night with him. My family had left Antrim and moved to Belfast. By the time I was eighteen, we were all travelling to the city for work, so it didn't make sense anymore, and we wanted to be in the city. David would come to see me at my parents' place, or I would stay with him at his parents' place. They owned a shop, and I would often help them out by working there. David became a part of our family. He was almost like another son to my mum. They all loved him, but they could see that he behaved possessively towards me.

At my best friend's wedding, I was having fun dancing with my dad, and David came over and said, "Your boobs are bouncing up and down, and people are looking."

I had started to come out of myself and develop my confidence. I have a fun personality, just like my dad, and I was simply expressing myself at a family gathering. He was twisting it into something else and trying to make me feel ashamed. Deep down, I knew this was not right.

We had many arguments, and many times we split up. This only ever lasted a few weeks, as he would bombard me with cards and teddy bears until I came back to him. Looking back now, I wish I'd possessed the strength to stay away. I guess I was also very insecure. I mistook his obsessive neediness for real love. I was afraid no one would ever love me like he did.

David seemed to be overly obsessed with my body. I had a beautiful body, but I was not that sexually driven. I didn't desire sex, but because he did, he was constantly pressuring me to perform this act. I began to dread it so much that it became very uncomfortable for me. He would say, "I love you so much. Please—just tonight, and I will let you off for a few days." He would buy me things and say, "In return, I want to have sex four times."

This didn't feel right to me. Why would I need to have sex in return for a gift? But I had never been sexually or romantically involved with anyone before him, so I had nothing with which to compare it.

At the time, I had no idea what was going on; all I knew was that it didn't feel right at all. I started to feel that what I wanted didn't count. I started to hate sex. Even having relatively little experience of it, I knew it was something

I really didn't need. I did love David, and I guess I loved how much love he showed me. Was his behavior towards me somewhat unhealthy and obsessive? I think so. Although David loved me and behaved generously towards me in certain ways, I simply knew this was not the kind of love I wanted. As the years rolled by and I matured, I began looking at other men and feeling attracted to them. Whenever I watched romcoms, I would wonder what it would be like to really fall head over heels for someone. At this point, I really should have walked away and never looked back, but I stayed with him. My insecurities kept me there. I believed no one else would ever love me like he did. I wish I had followed my instincts. If I could go back and rewrite anything in my life, this would be the thing that I would change.

When I was twenty-one, David proposed to me, and I accepted. Deep down, I knew I didn't want to get engaged; it was simply what I felt I had to do. I felt like I was living the life of a thirty-year-old woman. I yearned to be out enjoying life, traveling, and dating boys, like other girls my age. I started going out more frequently with my friends, and this fueled escalating arguments.

Finally, I decided I just couldn't do it anymore. I broke off our engagement and split up with him. At the time, I had been spending even more time at his parents' house, as I preferred being there to dealing with my mum's controlling and abusive behavior, which had become unbearable. Losing my sanctuary was one of the toughest aspects of the breakup.

After leaving David, I started modeling and doing motor shows. David had never wanted me to model, as he was so possessive of me. Now I had the freedom to live my life as I pleased. When I was signed to promote Peugeot at the Ulster Motor Show, I was so excited. At the show's launch I was photographed for the cover page of the Sunday World, lounging atop a swanky convertible in a pair of sexy white short shorts, a skintight white T-shirt, and a black leather biker jacket. The same image of me appeared on the cover of the Belfast Telegraph. People would come up to me and exclaim, "Denise! You're on the front of the Telegraph!"

I felt like a movie star. This was such a massive confidence boost for me, and I felt that I was making my mark in the world. Although the innocence of it all makes me laugh now, working at those shows and at many Bass Ireland promotions around Belfast was incredibly empowering. I became braver and more poised and self-assured. I felt comfortable revealing my flirty, fun side, and my real personality started to shine through.

And yet, David was never far away. He continued to linger in the background, and I kept going back to him and leaving again. I knew I was hurting him, but I couldn't help it. He loved me so much that I couldn't stay away. Looking back on it now, I realize I must have needed the security of having him near me. I simply could not go it alone. Whenever I tried to make it on my own, I would always end up falling back into my safety net. I was addicted to the way he loved me, even though it was slowly destroying us both.

A New Love

At twenty-two, I took out a bank loan to purchase a little white Peugeot 205 Open. It had a green tartan interior and was named after the French Open tennis tournament. Did I feel awesome in that car? I sure did. Best of all, it was costing me only £120 a month to pay it off. I had signed with ACA Models and was getting lots of modeling work in the evenings and at weekends, plus I worked full-time and still lived at home.

One evening, I spun the Peugeot through the city streets at sunset, with my friend Michelle riding shotgun. Michelle was a slim girl with a great sense of humor. We had grown up together through secondary school and we loved to dance the night away. I wasn't drinking, so I could drive on a night out. In the suede jacket and trousers I had purchased earlier that day, I felt like a supermodel.

We rocked up to the Wellington Park Hotel, which was the place to be seen in Belfast. Inside, people gathered around the various bars and in the lobbies while others paraded by. Everyone was chatting, flirting, and giving each other the eye. One part of the hotel had a DJ and a dance floor. This is where I could usually be found, shaking my hips like a mad thing, and working up a sweat to every Eighties song that came on. There would often be a lot of guys standing around and eyeing up the girls.

As I stood there with my fizzy drink in hand, chatting to Michelle and glancing around at the other patrons, I noticed a handsome guy in a baby blue shirt and jeans. He was looking in my direction. Over the course of the evening, he kept catching my eye. It simply wasn't my style to approach anyone, so the ball was in his court.

When Michelle said she wanted to leave, I said, "No problem—let's go."

As we walked out to the car park, I felt someone approaching me from behind and heard a man's voice. "I love your suit. My sister has the same one."

I turned around. It was the good-looking guy from the bar. Michelle kept walking, but I paused and replied, "Thank you."

"Where are you off to?" he asked with a smile. He had big brown eyes.

"We're heading home," I said, and continued walking to my car.

As I unlocked the car door, he said, "Where do you work?"

"Lumaset," I said, though I doubted he would be able to remember it.

"OK," he said. "Safe travels."

I got into the car and said to Michelle, "He was lovely, wasn't he?"

"Yeah," she said. "Now come on, drive."

The following Monday, I went to work as usual. In the middle of the morning, the phone rang, and I answered it. A somewhat familiar voice said: "Is this the girl with the suede suit?"

I nearly fell off my chair in surprise. "Yes, this is Denise," I said, pretending to maintain some semblance of calm.

"This is Joe," he said.

"I can't speak now," I told him. I gave him my number. "Call me later."

He phoned me at home that very evening, and this was how my second romance began. Joe was charming, fun, and extremely tall. He played rugby, and he was fairly obsessed with maintaining his looks and fitness. He came from the north coast of Antrim, so he would often bring me out to the clubs in Portrush, which was the place to be. Back then, Belfast city was not as it is now. Everything would close at night, so people my age would travel to Portrush at the weekends to attend various clubs. Tracks and Kelly's were the hottest places to go. Portrush was just over an hour's drive from Belfast, depending how fast you drove.

It was exciting to date someone new, as I had only ever been with David. When Joe came to pick me up before we headed out for the night, he always looked so handsome. I loved the scent of his aftershave. He had a country accent and worked in sales, so he had the gift of the gab.

At that time, I was still in regular contact with David. He couldn't handle the fact that I was with someone else, and I felt guilty for hurting him. I still had a strong bond with him and was scared to totally let go.

As Joe knew I was still speaking to David, he would ask me, "Do you still love him?"

"No, no," I would reassure him, "that's all over."

But of course, it wasn't. I felt so torn. I really fancied Joe. With him, sex was everything I had imagined it should be. But I could never get David out of my mind. Thanks to my self-doubt and insecurities, I still believed David was the only person who would ever really love me. Deep down, I knew that Joe loved women and sex, perhaps to the point that he would find it hard to be monogamous. I sensed that I could not trust him. Looking back, I see that my intuition was spot-on. I am like a witch—I can usually sense how things will turn out.

When Joe and I had been dating for around two months, I confessed that I was still in love with David. Joe was really hurt and attempted to prevent me from going back to David. I said, "I can't help the way I feel."

The next day, I arrived home from work at lunchtime to find Joe's car parked outside my parents' house. I stayed in my car and watched him leave.

When I went into the house, I asked my mum, "What was Joe doing here?"

She said, "He wanted to tell me how much he loves you and that he wants to marry you."

I was in shock. While I tried to figure out what I should do, my mum dropped another bombshell. She told me that David had also called that day to issue an ultimatum: Unless I agreed to marry him in six weeks, he would never take me back. Confusion swirled in my mind. What should I do? Should I risk it with Joe, who I didn't feel I could trust, or return to David, who I knew would never leave me? How did that old saying go? *Better the devil you know than the devil you don't.*

I was only twenty-two and had no desire to get married at this point in my life. I was happy just dating, but both of the men I loved were applying so much pressure to our relationships. I felt totally messed up. While I loved them each in a different way, I couldn't tell which of these was real love. I was so confused I didn't know where to turn. It seemed that no one could help me to make this decision.

My dad, who never got involved in my romantic issues, took me aside and told me, "You better be careful what you are doing. It's your life, and you have a long life ahead of you."

I wish I had heeded these words. But part of being young is that we don't always listen to those who are older and wiser than we are.

I was faced with a seemingly impossible choice, as I loved both men. When I look back on it now, I realize I may have been more in love with Joe. After much soul-searching, I came to a decision. I would marry David. I wrote Joe a card saying I was sorry for hurting him and drove up to the north coast to leave the card at his house, along with a CD of *The Bodyguard* soundtrack, which contains the Whitney Houston song "I Will Always Love You."

On the drive back home, I told myself: *David will love you and care for you the most. You have got to get Joe out of your head. He probably would have hurt you in the long run.*

The Big Day

My mum was delighted by the news that David and I were engaged again. She immersed herself in planning the big day. I didn't care to shop tirelessly for a wedding dress; I was happy with looking at just one. I chose it from a photograph and ordered it. When it arrived, I tried it on. It was perfect in every way, with fitted lace and a fishtail that grazed the floor. The slightly sheer bodice was covered with beautiful cream lace. It was very elegant, and I felt like a princess in it. My full-length veil sat perfectly atop my hair, which I wore in a bright blond bob.

    I bought my cream-colored shoes in a sale, and my mum made my sister's bridesmaid dress. We booked the Culloden Hotel in Cultra for the wedding reception, which cost my poor dad a small fortune. Though my parents wanted us to have a Catholic ceremony, David's family is Protestant, so his parents were in no rush to enter a chapel. Finally, we agreed we'd be married at St Anne's Cathedral, which is Church of Ireland, and therefore a more neutral choice.

On my wedding day, in the car on the way to the cathedral, I said to my dad, "I am not sure I'm doing the right thing. I'm only twenty-three. I don't really want to get married."

My dad was a very rational man, and he knew how to read people. He loved David and thought of him as a part of our family, but he was fully aware of David's flaws. He knew David was obsessed with me, and that his insecurities had made him very materialistic.

"Well," Dad said, "it's not too late. You can still cancel the wedding. Who cares about guests and costs? Just do what is right for you. Live your life as you wish."

For a moment, everything seemed crystal-clear. Yet the idea of calling off the wedding at the last minute filled me with terror and dread. I felt I simply had to marry David. I couldn't let him down. I would have to go ahead with it.

We had our fairytale wedding in St Anne's, a picture-perfect cathedral in the heart of the city. As I walked through the distinctive red doors, I spotted a few people we had not invited, who had shown up just wanting to catch a glimpse of me. It was very exciting, but I was so nervous. The newfound confidence I had acquired in recent years seemed to evaporate.

I remember clutching the crook of my dad's arm and walking down the seemingly endless aisle with my head bowed. As we approached the apse, I looked up to see David gazing at me with a blissful, open expression. He was so happy and delighted about our impending marriage. If I were to call everything off now, it would destroy him. I told myself: *You really do love him. Everything will be fine.*

The ceremony went smoothly. My best friend Andrea's mother sang, her beautiful voice backed by an amazing choir. The atmosphere was simply breathtaking. At the reception, when it was time for David to make his speech, the nerves suddenly hit him. He stood up and froze. He was simply paralyzed with fear.

I rose to my feet and said, "I will speak on behalf of my husband."

I proceeded to make a lengthy wedding speech although I was completely unprepared. Somehow the words and memories tumbled out effortlessly. People were smiling and laughing in all the right places. At the end, I saw a few people dabbing at their eyes with napkins. *Where did that come from?* I asked myself as I sat down. Perhaps I did possess an inner confidence that just needed to be let out. Perhaps I would shine in life after all.

I will never forget that day. David was in high spirits, as were all our guests. It had been a truly spectacular wedding and reception. The following morning, we headed off to Mauritius. I was tremendously excited that we would be spending our honeymoon in such a fabulous, far-flung location. The farthest away from Ireland I had ever traveled was to Spain and Greece. My excitement was unreal.

My first wedding - Culloden Hotel

Heaven

On our honeymoon we stayed in a five-star beach hotel. We befriended a couple from Newcastle who were staying at the same hotel. The wife was a very attractive woman in her thirties, and the husband, who was clearly punching above his weight, was a company CEO. We ended up spending a lot of time together and getting to know them. It was apparent that they enjoyed a great lifestyle, with all the perks.

One afternoon, as we were lounging on the beach drinking enormous, dreamy pink cocktails, she turned to me and said something I would never forget: "Marriage is hard enough when you love a person. Just imagine how hard it is if you don't."

Oh God, I thought. Her words seemed to echo in my mind. As I reflected upon my own situation, I asked myself: *Do I really love David enough to stay married to him? What have I done? Can I honestly picture spending the rest of my life with him?* Feeling my doubts and uncertainties beginning to spiral, I quickly pushed these thoughts to the back of my mind. I didn't want to think that far ahead, and I wasn't ready to entertain the thought that marrying David might have been a huge mistake.

We returned to Northern Ireland and got settled in the apartment that had formerly been David's bachelor pad. David's business continued to flourish. Over the years, my contribution was to spend my evenings balancing the books and helping him out in any way I could. Before long, we decided to build a house in Hillsborough. David found an old cottage on a parcel of land that encompassed twenty acres of beautiful countryside, and he set off planning the house. Hillsborough is a gorgeous location. It is home to Hillsborough Castle, where the Queen stays whenever she visits the area. It comprises a picturesque village surrounded by very affluent areas with stunning homes, restaurants, and gift shops.

Hillsborough is a predominantly Protestant town, so in those days Catholics were not permitted to buy land there. That was how life was back then, and I guess I had just gotten used to it. Our bid to purchase the property was accepted because David is Protestant and, because no one suspected me of being Catholic, we were able to pull the wool over their eyes.

As my maiden name is an English surname, and my dad was called Billy Robinson, people tend to assume I am Protestant. As a result, many people have unwittingly revealed their true nature to me. I have listened to many bigoted statements about how Catholics are smelly, don't wash, and never have any money. Over the years, having so many people openly share their prejudices with me has shown me whom I can trust. Yet for most of my life, I was secretive about my religious affiliation, for fear of not being liked or accepted. I deeply regret this now.

After a year of married life, we moved into our new home. David would not stop bragging about the mod cons and designer furniture. Although I found his self-aggrandizing behavior extremely boring and somewhat off-putting, I did love the house. We had two gorgeous chow dogs, and I had a pet goat.

When David bought me a horse, I was super excited. I had always wanted to ride. Gemma was a bay mare and was sixteen hands. We had a stable at the house, so I was able to take her for a hack along the country road and put her into the field. At night, I'd bring her into the stable. I was happy and content with all my animals around me. I adore animals and would have one of every species if I could.

There I was, living in the most scenic part of Northern Ireland and not wanting for anything, but I wasn't happy. I felt like I was being smothered by David's sexual needs. While I didn't crave sex or physical affection, he was still always pushing for it. This served only to increase my aversion to sex. Naturally, this caused all kinds of problems between us. As time passed, my sense of happiness and fulfilment continued to fade, and I began to socialize more in Belfast.

At this stage I was twenty-five. I was still working at Lumaset, but as I had begun selling print, I was spending quite a lot of time on the road and getting lots of male attention. I was still modeling and working at the motor shows, and David disapproved of this. I told him I loved modeling and planned to continue. Looking back, I can see that he was trying to keep me inside the proverbial gilded cage. He seemed to think that if he could buy me enough things, I would stop living the life I wanted. Instead, it drove me away. I was starting to feel really trapped.

One weekend, Andrea came to stay with me. She had gotten married and moved to Manchester, so I hadn't seen her in a few months. Andrea arrived on a Friday after work, and the two of us went out to Cutters Wharf. It is a fabulous bar along the Lagan in Stranmills, where everyone who was anyone would be seen. We got very drunk together and were having a grand time. Much later that evening, we ended up in the Wellington Park, where we ran into David.

He looked at me with disgust. "Look at the state of you," he hissed. "I'm ashamed to call you my wife. You're a disgrace."

I gazed into his eyes and calmly replied, "Ah—fuck off."

I walked away and left him to pick his jaw up off the floor. Andrea and I could not stop laughing, like two bold brats at school. I was reminded of our schooldays at the Whorehouse on the Hill.

We have been best friends since then, and we always will be. Our whole lives have run along parallel lines. We entered the workplace at same time and passed our driving tests at the same time. We met our first loves at the same time. And, as it turned out, we had both made the same mistake on that front.

When David and I had been married for three years, I realized how unhappy I was. I knew I was greatly loved, but that wasn't enough. I wasn't in love. I felt trapped. I wanted to fly and be free to live my life. As much as I dreaded inflicting any emotional pain upon David, I was twenty-six and I didn't want to wake up one day, aged thirty-six and still feeling this way. I knew I would have to leave him and start a new life. I needed an escape plan.

I began secretly hunting for a new place. I wanted David to keep the beautiful house we had built together, as he truly loved it. Eventually, I found a small apartment close to my parents' house. I purchased it without telling anyone. After completion, I knew I would have to tell David I was planning to leave him, but I couldn't find the right words. The weeks passed. It is incredibly hard to leave a person who loves you and is prepared to give you everything.

One morning as he was trying to initiate sex, I jumped out of bed, much to his surprise.

"That's it," I said. "I can't do this anymore. I need to get away."

"Don't say that! I love you," he said.

I went outside to clean the horse stable, and he came after me.

"You can't leave me," he said. "We can work things out."

"I can't," I said, choking on my words. I knew how much I was hurting him. "I need to be free. I bought an apartment, so you can keep the house. All I want is the horse and the goat and some personal items."

It was the hardest thing I ever had to do. He was my family. We had grown up together. When I spoke with David's mother about everything afterwards, I told her how I felt.

She said, "I respect you for being honest."

Many of our acquaintances were judgmental of my decision to leave David. Although I never tried to take the house and I didn't want any of his money, some people are prepared to believe the worst about you.

My dad said, "You can't stop people talking. They are strangers and what they think is of little importance. You're what's important."

I knew he was right. This was my life and my future, and I couldn't concern myself with other people's views.

I remember the day I left. As I walked away, I looked back at our splendid house, standing alone in the middle of the countryside. To me, it was bricks and mortar. A gilded cage. When I arrived at my little two-bedroom apartment, I was so happy. I closed the front door and told myself, *This is going to be painful, but you have made the move and now you are here. Start living the life you've always wanted.*

After David and I split up, we stayed in each other's lives for a while. We would meet up for dinner every so often. I thought it was a good idea to maintain the friendship, and I was still very attached to him. After some time, I realized I was only dragging out the pain of our separation, which wasn't healthy for either of us, so I eventually broke off contact with him.

I missed him so much, especially at first. We had been together for almost a decade. Apart from my short relationship with Joe, I knew nothing other than him. It felt as though I had lost my left arm. My parents loved David, so they stayed in contact with him. Whenever I heard he was dating someone new, I would feel very jealous. But no matter how much it hurt, it never hurt so much that I wanted to go back to him. I knew we both needed to move on.

 I had always wanted to be free. Even as a little girl, I never thought about getting married or having kids. I had my own dreams. Looking back now, I wish I had ventured out and lived those dreams. But my choices were influenced by fears and insecurities, stemming from my childhood. I needed love, so it was inevitable that I would first walk down the path that I believed would lead me to it.

Freedom

I started living my single life and enjoying my independence. Having recently been promoted, I was earning more money and driving a company car. I had my first sales job and was travelling around Northern Ireland selling print. It's a competitive field, but I thrived in it, as I loved engaging with new people every day. I established relationships with a few good companies, and business started to build.

My best friend, Andrea, had recently learned that her husband was having an affair. She had left him and moved back to Antrim, and at weekends she would come and stay with me in my new apartment in Belfast. We had both gotten married too young and were really starting our lives now. Belfast was changing. New bars and clubs were springing up everywhere, and the barriers were coming down. However, dating was tricky, as tensions between Catholics and Protestants remained high.

One night, we went to the Stormont Hotel in the east of the city. As it was in a predominantly Protestant area, many police officers in the RUC socialized there. It had a disco, and the music was fab. As usual, I danced the night away. At one point, a tall, handsome guy came over to me and started chatting me up. Eventually he asked me out, I accepted, and we arranged to meet the following week.

On our date, he kept asking me to say specific words. I knew exactly what he was doing. In those days, many people would attempt to guess your religion without directly asking you. As I had an English name, I wasn't that easy to read. I kept him guessing all evening, and at the end of the night I asked him if he thought I was Catholic.

"Of course not," he replied. "You don't look like one, and you don't smell."

"I am Catholic," I told him. "And I'm disgusted by what you said."

I walked away and left him there, staring at me like I had two heads.

As time went on, I started to really enjoy my new life. I was single, having fun with my friends, doing promotional work for Bass Ireland in the bars around the city, and modelling. I was always busy, and I couldn't wait for the weekend to come. Every Friday night, usually straight after work, I would go to Cutters Wharf with a group of my friends and colleagues. I loved it so much that I would be back again on Saturday, and sometimes on Sunday, depending on the hangover. My mum often said that I should move into Cutters Wharf. After about a year, there was a fire and it burned down. It has since reopened, but it no longer has the magic that it once had.

Around that time, I encountered my third love, Pete. He was blond, attractive, and fun, but he may have been a little too fond of the drink. We had way too many fights. It lasted about a year. We had shared some great times and a few holidays, so it wasn't all bad.

I was twenty-eight now, and I was having lots of fun and making new friends. I had become close with Alison, the owner of the modelling agency. She is stunning, statuesque, and has a very commanding presence. Everyone in the agency was scared of her, as she can be fierce and always speaks with such authority. Alison had won Miss Northern Ireland and was a Miss UK finalist before establishing her modelling agency and the Miss Northern Ireland Beauty Pageant. I never miss it—I reserve a table every year, and it is always a super night out.

I also became great friends with Judith, one of the Miss Northern Ireland winners. Judith is very tall and shy, with black hair and ivory skin. She reminded me of Snow White. We had some fun times together. Many a time, we would polish off a bottle of Goldschläger in an evening.

Through socializing around Belfast, I befriended a group of girls and guys who were all around my age. They had speedboats, so every Sunday we would go water-skiing and then head to Madison's, a hotel in town that hosted a nightclub on Sunday evenings. I loved that place. I could always be found there, dancing the night away. I enjoyed discovering all the bars and clubs in Belfast, and I loved my group of friends.

We started spending weekends in Dunfanaghy, a small town and former fishing port on the north coast of County Donegal. This is a regular spot for people from the North, many of whom have holiday homes there. We would spend the days water-skiing and while away the evenings in cozy Irish pubs, with open fires and fiddle-de-dee music.

I loved those weekends away. We had so much fun. Simple pleasures, such as walking the sand dunes, were super fun on those spectacular beaches. I would return home on a Sunday evening feeling exhausted yet exhilarated. On Monday morning when the alarm went off, I would feel ready to face a new week.

I was lucky. I had a lovely apartment, great friends, a good job, and a fancy car. I felt I had it all. Despite my packed schedule, I faithfully attended circuit classes and Boxercise to stay in shape, as I was drinking every weekend. I had started doing this only after I split up with David. We had occasionally had some wine in the evenings, but alcohol was not a feature of our life together. I guess my life had changed a lot.

Start of my modeling days – Belfast

Obsession

Before long, I fell for someone within my circle of friends. I loved MJ's cheeky sense of humor and his dark hair, huge brown eyes, and slightly cocky, ultra-confident swagger. I was immediately attracted to him. He had a stocky build and a perfect ass, as he played rugby and other sports, and he always wore Ralph Lauren shirts and blue jeans. I went out at weekends and would end up meeting him on most nights. The chemistry between us was off the charts. Sex with him was fantastic. I almost couldn't believe I had once been so ambivalent about sex.

Even once MJ and I had started hooking up regularly, we never thought to define our connection. And although I wasn't sure whether we were dating exclusively or not, he was everything to me. I wanted it to be only us. One weekend, he went away somewhere. I met up with my friends, as usual. I ended up chatting to a guy in pub, and this somehow got back to MJ.

When he confronted me about it, he was extremely angry with me.

I said, "We're not in a relationship, are we? What do you expect me to do? Am I meant to just hang around and wait for you?"

Since we had never discussed it, I was unsure of our status. He soon made it clear that he had assumed we were in a relationship, and he now felt I had been somehow disloyal. It seemed so unfair—I hadn't been the least bit interested in the other guy. He was only chatting me up, and I got chatted up all the time, so I hadn't thought much of it. When I tried to explain where I was coming from, MJ grew defensive and kept arguing with me. He said he could not trust me. That really hurt, especially as I knew I had done nothing wrong—he was just twisting it to make me feel bad.

After that, on the weekends I was out, I always hoped MJ would be in the bar. If ever he wasn't there, I would go looking for him. Although we still ended up together on many nights, I was aware that he was seeing other women. There were even nights when I would see him leaving the bar with some other woman. This really hurt me, but it did not deter me from loving him. Quite the opposite, in fact. The more he hurt me, the more I wanted him. It reached the point where I was obsessed with the desire to be with him. I wasted so many hours, crying over him. One of MJ's friends said, "If you would ignore him and not take him back, then he will come back to you properly."

Could I do that? Absolutely not. The more he rejected me, the more I wanted to be with him.

This was history repeating itself. The more my mum had shouted at me and belittled me, the more I had craved her approval. I did not recognize this at the time, so I continued to spend my nights crying over MJ. I wanted him to love me, but he kept toying with my emotions by stringing me along and flaunting his other relationships. I believe that he had strong feelings for me, but that he was quite messed up by his own family situation, so he was not ready to form a healthy relationship.

My friends implored me to stay away from him, but I couldn't. It was always the same story. I would start dating some lovely guy who would wine and dine me, and everything would be going well. Then, as soon as MJ heard I was seeing someone else, he would call me and say, "None of these guys are like me."

I would fall for it every time. I would break it off with the new guy and spend the night with MJ, and then he would treat me badly again.

My self-esteem was plummeting, but I couldn't break the cycle. It was like a drug—no one could stop me. I was addicted to him, and it was destroying me. The worse I felt, the more I needed him. This pattern mirrored my relationship with my mum, and that's why I couldn't recognize how unhealthy it was.

Having imprinted on my mum's abusive behavior, I had come to believe that love is never given freely, and that it always involves some degree of emotional pain. Because MJ's treatment of me felt so familiar, it felt like love. I thought it was up to me to make him love me. I accepted the way he treated me because I believed I was to blame. And even though MJ was causing me so much emotional pain and damage, I continued to try to win his affection. I told myself that he would change someday. But that day never came.

Eventually, my self-esteem hit an all-time low, and I finally realized I could not go on like this. Enough was enough. It was time to turn the page. I wanted to meet a nice guy and enjoy a fun and healthy relationship, instead of dealing with constant stress and anxiety. For my thirtieth birthday, I decided to have a party in a restaurant in Belfast. I didn't invite MJ, although I invited everyone in our shared circle of friends.

The party was such fun. All my friends were in fine form, and we ended up having an afterparty back at my apartment. MJ kept phoning me and asking to come over, but I stayed strong and held my ground that night. I was beginning to understand just how destructive our relationship was, but it would be some time before I learned to love myself enough to break the cycle.

As you may have guessed, this wasn't the end of our story. On more than a few occasions, I ended up with MJ at the end of the night. I could not resist him—the attraction was overpowering. When I look back at my thirty-year-old self, I can see that I had it all, though I didn't know it then. I was going from strength to strength in my career, and I was modelling and working at motor shows, including the London Motor Show. I drove a convertible Z3 and lived in a plush, newly built apartment. But I still didn't know how to love me.

Whirlwind

I spent much of that year trying to figure out how to be happy and get on with my life. I still missed my animals, and the peaceful country life I had known. I had the idea that if I were to get a dog and move out of the city, I would spend less time going out and socializing. Maybe that way I would be able to keep myself away from MJ. That was when I adopted Penny, my little black Pomeranian, from a dog rescue home. I sold my apartment and purchased a house in Saintfield, out in the countryside, around ten miles from Belfast.

One afternoon, I was sitting in the office contemplating this new chapter of my life, when I received a call from a number I didn't recognize.

"I'm at work, I'll have to phone you back," I said. "Who, may I ask, is speaking?"

"This is Justin."

Justin? I thought. *This boy has some set of balls!*

Flashback to a Friday night in Cutters Wharf a few years before. An older man had approached me while I was out with my friends. He appeared to be in his early forties, and he was extremely flirty and struck me as being rather arrogant. I remember feeling his hand on my ass and thinking he was being way too aggressive. My friend Sonia informed me that his name was Justin, and that he owned several companies in Belfast.

I replied, "I don't care if he owns Buckingham Palace! I don't like him."

A few days later, Justin had called me as I was driving home from work. "How did you get my number?" I demanded. "And why are you calling me?"

"Let's just say I got it from a mutual acquaintance. I want to take you out for dinner."

"No, thank you," I said, feeling slightly creeped out. He had likely acquired my number under false pretenses. "I have a boyfriend."

Though I wouldn't have called MJ my boyfriend, I knew this was the best way to turn down guys like Justin.

"OK, no problem," Justin had said. "No doubt I'll see you around."

I had ended the call, thinking, *Not if I see you first!*

Sure enough, I had bumped into Justin on two different occasions about a month later. The second time, he was rather inebriated. Though I still wasn't interested in him, he was all over me like a cheap blanket. Fortunately, MJ happened to be in the bar that night, so we left together and that was that. Or so I had thought.

Until now. Here I was, almost thirty-one, sitting at my desk, with the boy himself at the other end of the line.

"Let me take you out for lunch," Justin coaxed. "Come on, we'll have a laugh."

I was a proud new dog owner, preparing to leave city life behind. But it was a sunny bank holiday weekend, and I hadn't made any plans. And to be honest, I was still hurting over MJ.

"Yeah, OK," I said.

Why not? It was only lunch.

We met at a restaurant near my place. When I saw him, I thought, *He's not nearly as bad looking as I had thought.* He's bald, almost six foot tall, and very lean, with clear blue eyes. Over lunch, we got to know each other a little better. He told me he had two children from a previous marriage, and that he had recently come out of a relationship. He seemed every bit as brash and forward as I had remembered, but he revealed another, more positive aspect—a sense of daring and mischief.

As I left the restaurant, I thought, *There's something about him that is really attractive.*

I didn't know what it was at the time, but I can see it now. He's extremely assertive, and I had never dated anyone with this type of character.

As soon as I got home from our date, Justin phoned. He suggested going for a walk with our dogs the following day. I thought, *Gosh, he is keen.*

I looked around my apartment. I would be moving house in a week, so a lot of my things were already packed in boxes and the whole place was upside down. But I quite liked the idea of the two of us walking our dogs together, so I agreed to go.

His young Saint Bernard was huge, gorgeous, and full of energy, but she was no match for my pint-sized Pomeranian. Penny kept trying to bite the ass of the Saint Bernard. You know how they say that inside every small man is a much bigger man, fighting to get out? The same applies to dogs.

This marked the beginning of the next chapter in my life. It was a whirlwind romance. Justin kept whisking me off to all kinds of exciting destinations. I barely had time to pack my bags, much less to breathe.

When I learned that Justin's marriage had broken up because he was having an affair with his secretary, I found this all quite predictable. At least, that's what I thought, or what he manipulated me to think. There were a few evenings when I couldn't get him on the phone, and I sometimes wondered exactly how final this breakup had been. I wanted to be happy, so I took everything he told me at face value.

Whatever was going on behind my back, I assumed it was over when he booked us a skiing holiday in Val d'Isère. Prior to this, I had been on two ski trips, during which I had not done any skiing. The first time was with David and the second time was with a few girlfriends, and I had spent the time eating lunch, drinking wine, and watching other people ski, as it really wasn't my type of holiday. It frightened me and my fear of breaking a leg outweighed any fun I might have. I preferred the après-ski.

When Justin booked the skiing trip, I thought, *Jeepers, I don't want to make an idiot out of myself by sitting there and drinking wine. I should make an effort to actually ski.* The idea was daunting.

We arrived at our hotel, which lay nestled at the bottom of the slopes and right in the town. Val d'Isère is a real party ski resort and one of the best. Justin is a party animal. He has bundles of energy, and this is partly why I fell for him. I loved his get-up-and-go attitude. He believes that nothing lies beyond his reach and that everything is possible. He comes from a farming background, so he isn't afraid of hard work, and that is another thing I have always admired about him. At age fifteen, he was already signing cheques on his parents' farm. He has a knack for business and an amazing work ethic. And, as the saying goes, he works hard and plays hard.

On our first day on the slopes, he brought me up the mountain.

Green runs are for novices, blue runs are for beginners, red runs are for intermediate skiers, and black runs are for experienced skiers.

I said, "I can only ski the blue runs."

"Yep, no problem," he said. "Let's do that."

When we jumped off the ski lift, I was totally unaware of the color of the run. Once I started skiing downhill, I could see the drop.

"This is a red run!" I shouted.

Justin shouted back, "Come on! It's not red, it's blue."

I tried to keep skiing, but then I stopped again and could not move.

"You fucker!" I yelled. "It's a black run!"

He said, "Will you stop looking at colors and come on?"

"No!" I screamed. "I'm not moving!"

I was scared for my life. I looked down the mountain and thought, *That's it, my number's up. I am about to die.* My legs were like jelly. I couldn't move. There was no way I was making it down that run.

After I had cried, squealed, and called him every choice name under the sun, he finally walked back up to me with his skis off. I was petrified. My boots were stuck in the snow, as I had removed my skis in fear of sliding down and being unable to stop. All I could hear was the swish of the other skiers flying past me at high speed. I was terrified, and all Justin could do was laugh.

I said, "If I make it home alive, you are dead."

After about an hour, I realized I had no choice but to try and get down the mountain with the full aid of Justin. By the time we finally reached the next lift, I think he fully regretted having thrown me in the deep end. But this was Justin all over. Without time to spare, he wanted me to be flying down the sides of mountains with him, so he thought he would speed up my learning by scaring the hell out of me on a black run on my first day.

Seeing as his sink-or-swim tactics hadn't succeeded, Justin arranged for me to have private lessons in the morning while he bombed happily down the mountainside, and then he taught me in the afternoons. As Justin has no fear of anything, he is a fabulous skier. He can even ski backwards, as I had observed while he was getting me down that first run. As the week progressed, I found myself enjoying it, and I started to pick it up really well. I guess there was some method in his madness. After many holidays, I am now a great skier.

Interlude

During the early days of my courtship with Justin, I was receiving many calls from MJ. Now that he couldn't have me, he wanted me back. I don't believe he really wanted to be with me; he simply didn't want anyone else to have me. Justin was well known in Northern Ireland because of his businesses, so MJ knew of him and did not like the idea that I was dating him. MJ would ring my house late at night and when I answered, he would hang up. Often, Justin would be there, and he would get annoyed. Justin was aware that MJ and I had seen each other on and off, but he didn't know exactly how long it had been going on or how badly MJ had messed me around.

Even though I was falling for Justin, I still had feelings for MJ. That magnetic pull was still there. When I first started seeing Justin, I had met up with MJ a few times.

When Justin and I started getting more serious about each other, I told MJ, "I have met a fun guy who wants to date me and treat me right, so you can jog on."

But the late-night phone calls carried on.

One day, when I was having coffee with MJ, he turned to me and said, "I miss you. Maybe we should go away for a weekend and see how things go."

I said, "I can't, I'm dating Justin now. But let me think about it."

I was tempted to go away with MJ. I wanted to know whether there was still something between us. We had a lot of history together, and I still fancied him so much. I told Justin I needed some time to think about what I wanted. Being the control freak that he was, he didn't like this one bit. Ever since our first date, he had consumed my life, though I didn't see it at the time.

I arranged to get away and I said to MJ, "OK, let's go to Dublin for the weekend."

We headed off to the fair city in my Z3 convertible. It was a sunny day, so we drove the hundred miles to Dublin with the top down. When we arrived at the hotel, my hair looked like a bird's nest, and I was quite sunburnt. We checked into the hotel and went up to our room, where I made myself appear somewhat normal again. Then we went straight to Temple Bar, where we spent the day on a pub crawl. We got so drunk.

By then, I had already started having real feelings for Justin, so I didn't enjoy being with MJ as much as I thought I would.

After we came back, I said to MJ, "I'm going to make a go of it with Justin, so please leave me to it."

He didn't, of course, but I had let go of him. I had finally gotten him out of my system.

Daredevil

Amidst all this dating, moving house, and going on holiday, I had also changed jobs. I was now working at a small family firm in Belfast, and I was doing well for myself there. I had acquired some great customers and managed to secure some big contracts. Justin moved into my place, as he had sold his house and was waiting for completion on his new house.

One day, he said, "Do you mind me parking my Porsche 911 in your garage? I don't drive it a lot."

I said, "Yeah, OK."

And just like that, I was in a full-blown relationship again, and I hadn't even come up for air.

Justin thought I was sexy, and he had quite a high sex drive. At times, I wondered whether Justin and his former secretary had had lots of sex. I had become more experienced and interested in sex, but I still hated being pressured to perform, like a seal at the circus. I liked sex, but I wasn't obsessed with it.

After Justin and I had been together for about three months, I discovered I was pregnant.

What am I going to do? I asked myself. *I don't want to have kids, and I'm not even sure if Justin is the right man for me.*

I felt so messed up and confused. I rang Andrea, and she came with me to the doctor's office. The doctor confirmed that I was indeed pregnant. I was so scared. But when I imagined that I might have a little girl, having a baby started to seem like a good idea.

A month later, I had a miscarriage. Although I wasn't sure whether I wanted to have a baby, when that happens, it really does make you wonder what it would be like. I think Justin was secretly relieved that he didn't have to go through all that again. Afterwards, I didn't dwell on what had happened. I felt it simply was not meant to be. I wasn't ready for it anyway.

Justin and I continued our relationship. He was controlling me, though at the time I didn't realize it. Looking back now, I can see it was all on his terms. I guess this is often the case with a powerful man, who is used to getting everything he wants. I was just another thing he wanted to possess. The first time we met, he had told me he was going to marry me. I had laughed out loud, thinking he was a little cocksure. He had said, "I always get what I want."

I was attracted to him because of his confidence. Ultimately, it was one of the characteristics that made me fall in love with him. Justin is a daredevil, a great skier and race car driver. You will find him doing anything that involves adrenaline. I loved his high-energy, ballsy attitude to life. I had the feeling that nothing could ever stand in his way.

One sunny Saturday morning, Justin and I woke up together at my place in Saintfield. Over a leisurely breakfast, we spoke about our plans for the day. He was going kart racing, I was meeting my friend Sonia, and I would meet up with him in the evening for dinner at a fabulous new restaurant in town. I told

Justin I didn't like it when he went kart racing, as I felt it was dangerous. But it was like talking to the wind. For him, danger wasn't a drawback—it was the whole point. The more danger something involved, the more he wanted to do it.

In the afternoon, I met up with Sonia on the Lisburn Road, an extension of Belfast's Golden Mile. The BT9 postal code denotes a beautiful neighborhood alongside the Malone Road, which is home to some of Belfast's most expensive properties. This is Belfast's version of Rodeo Drive, lined with luxury cars and ladies who lunch. While there are a lot of phony and pretentious people who hang out there, it's a glamorous and fun place to be, and I like the vibe.

Most Saturdays we would meet there for lunch and then go shopping in the lovely little boutiques, often bumping into various friends and acquaintances, and stopping to chat. Sonia is a funny girl with a huge personality. She's a blonde who looks a little like Stevie Nicks. A smooth-talking Mercedes Benz dealer who could have sold snow to an Eskimo, Sonia knew absolutely everyone.

We had a lovely time, catching up on each other's news over lunch, and trying on clothes and shoes in our favorite shops. When I arrived back at home, I unpacked my new outfit. As I was getting ready for my dinner date with Justin, I received a call on my mobile from a number I didn't recognize.

A man said, "Hello? Is this Denise?"

"Yes," I said. "Who's this?"

"I'm a friend of Justin's. I'm sorry to say he has been in an accident."

My heart felt like it was breaking into a million pieces. I could barely speak. "What? Where is he? Is he OK?"

"He's at Downpatrick Hospital."

"OK," I said. I took a deep breath. "I'll be there as soon as I can."

Downpatrick is about twenty-five minutes' drive from Saintfield. I jumped into my two-seater convertible and raced all the way there at breakneck speed. My heart was in my throat and my mind was spinning. All I could think of was how much I loved him. I could not stand the thought of losing him.

When I arrived at the small country hospital, I went straight to A&E. I could hear a man screaming in agony. I told the nurse who I was looking for, and she led me to him. As we neared the room where Justin was, I realized the bloodcurdling screams I'd been hearing were his. I started crying and couldn't stop.

Justin's son was waiting outside. He is a lovely, kind boy. He said, "They told me my dad crashed into another guy."

I said, "OK, thanks. I am going to try and go in and see him."

Just then, the door to the room opened and a doctor came out. I tried to run past him and into the room.

The doctor said, "Sorry, you'll need to wait outside."

"Please, no," I begged. "I need to see him."

"Why don't we step outside and have a chat?" The doctor guided me into the hallway. "He has broken a few of his ribs and some of his fingers and punctured a lung, but he's going to be fine. We're transferring him to Belfast City Hospital."

I breathed a sigh of relief. "OK, that's good to know. I'll follow them."

I jumped back into my car and tailed the ambulance down the winding country roads. As I was driving, I received a call. It was David. *I wonder what he wants*, I thought. "Hi," I said. "What's the craic?"

"Oh my God, I'm so sorry, Denise," he said.

"Why are you sorry? What are you talking about?" I asked, thinking, *Why would he apologize to me out of the blue?*

"You don't know? I'm the person who collided with Justin."

"Wait—what?" I couldn't believe what I was hearing. "How did this happen?"

"I went out of control, and Justin crashed into me."

"I mean, how were you even racing together?"

"Oh, I bought a kart and started racing some time ago."

Small world we live in. What are the odds of my ex-husband and my boyfriend racing against each other?

"Don't worry," I said, once I had wrapped my mind around it. "It's not your fault."

Still, David felt very badly about what had happened. He even visited Justin while he was in hospital.

Justin made a full recovery, and life returned to normal. I was madly in love with him and fully committed to our relationship. I especially loved his sense of adventure and spontaneity.

He would phone me at work on a Thursday and say, "I'm taking you out to dinner tonight. The table is reserved at five. I'll see you after work."

Later that evening, we would be having champagne and the craic, and he would say, "Let's stay in a hotel in town instead of going home."

We had so much fun together. He was exciting to be around. I admired his drive, his ballsiness, and his confidence. I respected him for having built his empire through hard work. I loved the fact that he was successful yet remained so down-to-earth.

After Justin had been staying with me for some time, his house purchase finally came through and I moved in with him. I let my house sit furnished and vacant for a while until I was ready to rent it out.

We kept a full social calendar. We attended lavish events and dinners with his colleagues and business contacts, and his connections at various banks would wine and dine us. We had lunch with some people from Bank of Ireland at a top restaurant in Belfast. It was such an extravagant lunch, with wine and champagne flowing freely. We carried on until two o'clock in the morning. By that time, I could barely string together a sentence. I had such a bad hangover the next day, I don't think I even made it out of bed.

One year into the relationship, our life was a constant stream of parties and nights out. We were drinking a lot, but I loved it and thought I was in heaven. The sex was amazing and awakened in me a new level of desire. The fire that burned within Justin seemed to be equal parts passion and jealousy. The more he loved me, the less he wanted any other man to speak to me. Whenever men would try to chat me up, I would turn them down because I was never interested in anyone but Justin. He could not see this, so we would have a huge fight and I would end up going to my vacant house to spend the night alone. When someone does not trust you, I think it's often a sign that they don't trust themselves.

The next day, he would apologize, and I would forgive him. His love was overbearing and controlling, like my mum's and David's, except it was much more intense and exciting. It bonded me to him. I could not bear to think about leaving him.

In the summers Justin would take his son and his daughter to Portugal, where he has a beautiful and spacious apartment in the Algarve. When Justin and I had been dating for a year, he invited me to join them. I had met them only a few times and had found them to be gorgeous kids. As daunting as it seemed, I was honored and excited to be part of their family vacation.

We rented a car that we nicknamed *the jalopy*, as it was a grey estate car that paled in comparison with the luxury cars that Justin usually drove. The holiday was fabulous, and we all had a great time together. We went to the water parks, and even swam with dolphins. I had fun with his kids. I am not precious, and I'm happy to dance around and act the eejit. I think his kids liked my personality and authenticity.

While I have never wanted to have my own children and don't regret that part of my life at all, I just loved Justin's kids. Their mum and dad had brought them up well, so they both already understood the value of money. While they had never wanted for anything, they never demanded or expected anything. They appreciated everything they had. They are truly lovely, down-to-earth, genuine people.

Over time, Justin became ever more possessive. Still, I tried to make sure that I had my own life while sharing my life with him. I would go out with my girlfriends on one night at the weekends. I love my girlfriends, and it is extremely important to me to nurture my friendships and make time for them. Whenever I went out with the girls, he would constantly check up on me. At first, I thought this was great. In my innocence, I believed this meant he truly loved me. But I came to understand that this was an attempt to control me. Although I never gave him any reason not to trust me, it's possible that he didn't trust himself, and that's why he didn't trust me.

One evening, we attended a ball at the Belfast City Hall. It was a very grand affair, and I was wearing a sleek new gown. Justin loved it when I dressed super sexy. Men have always sexualized my large breasts, so I always want to hide them, but Justin encouraged me to wear low-cut, tight-fitting dresses that showed off my cleavage and my curves. Justin loves to dance almost as much as I do, and we had taken over the dancefloor as usual. I was in a loved-up, sexy mood and feeling good about myself.

Being a risktaker, Justin often wanted to have sex in semi-public places where we might get caught. That day, while everyone else was in the ballroom enjoying the event, he convinced me to go into the accessible restroom with him to have sex. I liked it when he pushed the boundaries of my more modest sexual desires, so I went along with it, and I did enjoy the excitement.

Later, I noticed that Justin was flirting a lot with a tall, striking blonde. He often flirted with other women, but usually it didn't bother me, as I knew he loved me. This time, it started to irk me.

I remember saying, "Hey, will you stop flirting with her?"

"Ah, stop," he replied. "I'm only being friendly."

As the evening progressed, he kept going back and forth between the two of us.

At one point, the tall blonde turned to him and said, "Do you not think you should go back over to your beautiful girlfriend?"

I was so angry with him that night. More than that, I was hurt. For the first time in our relationship, I began to fear him. I wondered whether he was genuine and if I could trust him. Even viewed in the best possible light, his behavior was deeply disturbing because it betrayed a lack of respect for me. Even if he'd had no intention of hurting me, once I spoke up, he should have checked his behavior, instead of acting completely oblivious to my discomfort and humiliation. I wondered if I could spend my life with someone who made me feel so alone, even when we were together.

We went home and got into a horrible argument. What had started as a brilliant evening would now be etched into my memory, for all the wrong reasons. As always, Justin apologized the following day and made it up to me by being super nice. And as always, I forgave him. But a crack had appeared beneath the surface. I began to question our relationship, and to consider leaving him. I believe he sensed this, but he knew exactly how to manipulate my emotions for his own benefit. In the end, I always succumbed to his charms.

Dublin

Justin and I went on holidays and skiing trips together, and we always had great fun. He would also travel a fair bit without me. I was holding down a full-time job, so I couldn't keep taking time off. Besides, I enjoyed having time for myself.

I was always very respectful of his right to explore his favorite pastimes. I encouraged him to attend various Grands Prix and go skiing with his friends. I trusted him. During these trips, he would check in regularly, so I felt I had no reason to doubt him. I was happy he was doing what he loved to do, which tended to involve bombing down a mountainside at breakneck speed or indulging his petrolhead fantasies at a Grand Prix.

Meanwhile, I was having fun being a free spirit and spending time with my mates on evenings out in Belfast and weekends in Dublin. I would go on girls' trips to Dublin with Nuala, Sonia, and Andrea. We would always stay at the Burlington Hotel and dance the nights away in the club downstairs. I loved our chatty brunches and epic shopping sprees. Our hangovers were legendary.

When I was in Dublin, I would sometimes reminisce about the family holidays we'd had there. When I was growing up, we spent a lot of time in Dublin, as my aunts (on my dad's side) had all moved to the capital to escape the Troubles. We would always visit in the summer. My dad loved bringing us to all the historic sites. I remember visiting Kilmainham Gaol, Dublin Castle, Glasnevin Cemetery and many other points of interest. When my dad brought us to Christ Church Cathedral, where the Crusaders are buried, the guide asked us whether we would like to see the coffins containing their preserved bodies. He said they were in the crypt. I eagerly made my way to the front of the crowd.

"Get back here," my dad said. "It's not for kids."

I remember feeling so gutted.

I loved those trips. They were always so exciting. Compared to Belfast, Dublin seemed to be this huge, amazing city. On the long car journeys, my dad always played cassette tapes of Irish music. My siblings and I would fight over the center seat, as this provided the best view of the road ahead.

When Justin and I had been together for two years, he went on an overnight business trip to Dublin. He came back the next day and handed me a shopping bag from Brown Thomas, Dublin's most luxurious department store. I was thrilled.

"What's this?" I asked.

"Just open it," he said.

I wondered what it could be. As I tore open the wrapping paper, I saw the Louis Vuitton logo emblazoned on the box.

"You're always talking about these handbags," Justin said, smiling. "It's about time you had one."

My first Louis Vuitton handbag! I was over the moon. It was an Alma, whose lineage traces back to the Art Deco original named for the Alma Bridge in Paris. I admired its classic, elegant structure and the iconic Monogram motif. I was ecstatic. Justin seemed pleased by my reaction. That evening, when we went out for dinner, I carried my new handbag with pride. I felt like a movie star.

Colorado

The Millennium was approaching.

Justin said to me, "Seeing as this is a special year, let's go away together for two weeks. We'll leave on Boxing Day and celebrate New Year and our birthdays away."

Our birthdays fall one day apart in the first week of January.

"That sounds fantastic," I said. "Where are we going?"

"I thought we could go to Colorado to do a bit of skiing," Justin said. "We'll spend one week in Aspen and one week in Vail."

I knew these exclusive resorts are frequented by celebrities and the ultra-wealthy. *Imagine little old Denise from Antrim in such fabulous surroundings*, I thought, feeling quite overwhelmed.

When I told my mum, she said, "This man is spoiling you."

"I know," I said. "It's amazing, all the places he's taking me and all the exciting things we do."

I was on top of the world. I was with a man I loved and fancied, and we had so much fun together. My whole life felt like a dream.

Upon landing in Colorado, we rented a large four-by-four, with chains on the wheels. The snow-covered roads seemed dangerous to drive on, but Justin navigated them fearlessly. We arrived in Aspen late at night. Our hotel was prettily lit with elaborate Christmas decorations. Blanketed in snow, it looked picture perfect—exactly like a Christmas card. The hotel was very chic, and we had a fireplace in our room. It was marvelously romantic. I felt so special.

We were staying at The Little Nell, a five-star, five-diamond hotel with ski-in, ski-out facilities. When I looked out the window of our hotel room, I could see the ski lift right outside. We were assigned a personal valet, who carried our skis to the lift. How unreal is that? It felt weird to have people lifting and laying me like this, but I supposed this was the kind of treatment the hotel's clientele expected. Even then, I hadn't quite grasped the extent of Justin's wealth. I saw him as this madman who was always bursting with energy, who made me laugh and treated me like a princess.

In the morning we went downstairs for breakfast. We were sitting there, looking out at the slopes, when Justin said, "Guess who just walked in."

"Who?" I asked, scanning the room.

"Over there," he said. "Be cool."

It was Cameron Diaz. She's my favorite actress, so I went into shock for a moment. As soon as I was able to breathe normally again, I was dying to run over and say hello to her.

"Don't you move," Justin said. "In this type of hotel, people give them their space."

"Of course," I said, coming to my senses. "You're right, I understand."

I was totally starstruck. In her fur coat, with that trademark blond hair, she looked dazzling. She's smaller than she seems in her films. Then, as we were leaving the restaurant, Jean-Claude Van Damme walked in. I was just about having a heart attack from seeing all these famous people around our hotel. It was amazing. I felt like I was on another planet.

We headed out to ski. It was an extremely cold day. I was wearing thermals, goggles, and a balaclava. My toes were frozen after an hour.

I said to Justin, "This is not like Europe! It's too cold."

It was beautiful, but jeepers—it was tough.

Aspen is truly stunning. I was overwhelmed, if I am honest. We had dinner in town every evening. At times, I could barely take in all the opulence and grandeur. I kept thinking how lucky I was to be there. On New Year's Eve, the hotel hosted a spectacular Millennium Ball. We went by ourselves, but we chatted with lots of other people. Justin is exactly like me—he would talk to dogs in the street. We got to know a few of the other hotel guests and went for drinks with them after the dinner.

After ringing in the New Year at midnight, Justin and I went up to the bar and he ordered a bottle of champagne. I said to myself, *I can't drink anymore, I have had enough,* but I went along with it anyway. After we had returned to our table, Justin turned to me and held up his glass of champers. "Denise, will you marry me?"

I almost fell off my chair. "Oh my God!" I exclaimed. "This is a surprise."

I was caught completely off guard. *Jeepers,* I thought, *I don't really want to get married right now. But I do love him, and I don't want to be without him.*

"Yes, of course I will," I replied. "But let's not do it right away. Like, in a few years, if that's OK with you."

Justin blinked. "So maybe next year, then."

I said, "Maybe the year after."

"OK," he said.

He didn't have a ring, as he had wanted to ask me first.

I remember going to bed that night and thinking, *I am not staying long in the single life, am I?* Then I thought, *I should feel fortunate that he loves me so much. And I love him, so what is my problem? I need to wise up. I do want to marry him.*

We spent the second week of the holiday in Vail, which is two hours' drive from Aspen. Our hotel was styled like a log cabin and was as superb as The Little Nell. As soon as we arrived, I started to feel sick. My condition grew steadily worse over the course of the day, and it soon transpired that I had contracted a virus. I had to stay in bed that entire week. I was sicker than I ever had been in my life, and it was so frustrating—such a waste of money. Poor Justin had to ski on his own every day, and I missed out on celebrating my thirty-second birthday. Despite this debacle, it was the holiday of a lifetime. It was truly magical.

I was blissfully in love with Justin, but I wasn't in a hurry to get married again.

I told him, "I never want to go through another divorce. If we get married, this is it for me. I want us to last forever. Please don't ever hurt me."

"Of course," he said. "I know that. I will never hurt you."

Spring

After we returned home, I remained sick for another two weeks. By the time I recovered I had lost approximately fifteen pounds. As I had not been carrying any extra weight in the first place, I was much too skinny afterwards. Then it was back to work and the usual routine.

Things were going well in my career. I was making great money doing something I enjoyed. I continued to bring in important clients and I was rewarded for my hard work. My new company car was a brand-new black BMW convertible with cream leather upholstery. I was in love with it.

At weekends we often went to Justin's lake house in Fermanagh, home to the Lakelands, which are world-renowned for their breathtaking waterways. Having recently acquired a new print contract with a telecoms company, I had become friends with two of the women who worked there: Kathy, and Beverley. The three of us often went out for dinner together in Belfast.

Once Justin and I got to know Kathy and her husband, they would often come down to the lake house with us and our other friends. We would water-ski and jet ski all day, have a barbecue on one of the little islands, and then come back to the lake house for drinks and fun. On Monday morning, we would drive back up to Belfast and head to work.

On weekends when we weren't at the lake, I would go and help Justin's dad on the farm. All the little lambs were so adorable. I would bring some of them home to feed, as their mums had passed away. I had a great relationship with Justin's dad. He had been very successful in business as well, but he still loved working on the farm. I spent many Sundays there, grabbing the haylage for the cows and feeding the lambs.

At half past eight on a Sunday morning, we were in bed dying with a hangover from the night before, when the doorbell rang. It was Justin's dad.

"Come on up for your work," he said.

God, I thought, *I feel so bad. I'll be useless today*. I got up and said, "I'll be on my way!"

He seemed to enjoy my company.

I remember Justin saying, "You see what you have started now. This will be every Sunday."

I didn't mind at all. Being around the animals made me feel peaceful and happy. I wanted to look after them the best I could, as I knew their lives would be short.

One day, I was watching a calf being born. She got stuck, so they had to pull her out, and her leg got broken in the process. Justin and I went over there every evening to feed her and change her plaster. She was grey and had massive eyes. We couldn't let this little baby die. We went there every day for weeks, until she got better. She lived for many years.

Summer

As summer drew near, Justin started planning our vacation. He suggested going to Marbella for two weeks in July and bringing his kids. I told him that was a nice idea, so he set about making all the arrangements. We headed off and were having a wonderful time. I enjoyed Justin's kids a lot, and we always had great fun together.

One evening, we went out for dinner in a charming restaurant on the beach. I noticed that the kids appeared exceptionally happy and excited, which was lovely. It was a classy place with well-heeled clientele. It even had a singer, and a dancefloor. As we were ordering, a bottle of champagne arrived at our table. Justin's daughter was grinning like a Cheshire cat. Next thing I knew, Justin was down on one knee, presenting me with a ring and proposing to me in front of his kids, who clearly loved having been in on the secret.

I was blown away. I said, "Yes! Of course!"

As we got up to dance, the singer announced our engagement, and everybody cheered. It was embarrassing but also very special and romantic.

"Let's get married at Christmas," Justin said.

"What's the hurry?" I asked.

"Why wait?" he replied.

Even though I would have loved to spend more time just dating him, I was grateful to have such a kind and romantic man in my life. I also loved his kids, so I felt very fortunate and happy.

When we returned home, everyone was so excited for us. My friends helped me get started with the wedding plans. As Justin is Protestant, and as we had both been previously married, we opted for a civil ceremony at Belfast City Hall. We would have our wedding reception at my friend's award-winning restaurant, Shu. I started to get incredibly excited about everything. Justin was arranging a spectacular honeymoon, the details of which were to be kept secret until closer to the time.

Although I had never dreamed of getting married, here I was, about to embark upon my second marriage at the age of thirty-two. From the time we are very young, we are told that love is going to be like a fairytale, and Justin had come along and swept me off my feet with his romantic gestures. It was utterly intoxicating to be courted, showered with gifts and surprises, and whisked off to faraway lands.

Only later did I realize that he had taken over my life from our very first date. I can look back now and see what was really going on, but I was naïve at the time. I did not know who I was or how to fully love myself, so I felt that his love and attention defined me.

Deep down, I knew he was a flirt and that he had been unfaithful in past relationships. Although I sometimes feared that one day he would betray me as well, most of the time I felt safe in the assumption that he had learned from his mistakes. Most of all, I believed he really loved me.

Happiness

While I was busy planning our wedding, I had a lot going on at work. I had taken on some sizeable accounts, so every day was a race to meet all kinds of deadlines. Printing is an extremely demanding industry, and we were under constant pressure to get jobs turned around very quickly. I thrive in this environment, as I love rising to challenges and keeping my customers happy. I worked in a small, family-run business and I had been promoted to sales manager, so there were never enough hours in the day.

Over dinner one evening, Justin mentioned that we would be going on a six-week, round-the-world honeymoon.

"Six weeks? You know I can't take that much time off work," I said.

"Don't worry," Justin replied, "I have already spoken with your boss."

I was shocked that he would do this behind my back. I am very committed to my work, so I would never want to let my customers down in any way. "You can't do that," I told him. "I don't want to go away for six weeks."

He tried to explain why we needed to go away for such a long time. "Anyway," he added, "your boss was fine about it."

"No, you manipulated him," I said. "You should have asked me first."

That was Justin. Whatever he wanted, he would get. And I, too, had fallen in line. I always did exactly as he wanted.

"We have two dogs. How will they cope?" I asked him.

"They'll be fine. They can go into the kennels."

I wasn't happy about any of this. I knew Penny, my little Pomeranian, would miss me so much, and that Justin's Saint Bernard would feel the same.

Justin told me we were going to visit so many places and do so many fabulous things. It would be the holiday of a lifetime, and we would be flying everywhere in business class. How could I turn this down? It was a dream come true.

Now that I had been with Justin for two and a half years, I was growing accustomed to his extravagant lifestyle. I wasn't all that conscious of how extraordinary other people might find it—I was simply enjoying my life with him and didn't see myself differently. I was still little Denise from Antrim.

I didn't feel any different on the inside, either. My demons still tortured me. I always put myself down and ridiculed myself. When someone paid me a compliment, I didn't know how to accept it. I would wonder whether the person was being genuine. I always went straight for the negative.

Around this time, I became very good friends with a woman called Jude. She came across as somewhat aloof, so some of my friends wondered what I had in common with her, but we got on like a house on fire. She was a lot of fun once you got to know her. We often went out for dinner with friends of hers from the motor trade. We always had great craic when we got together, and we spent some late drunken nights in the city.

Jude had a high-powered job and earned a lot of money, which she loved to splash out on designer clothes. I could never understand this, as I love a bargain. I wondered why anyone would buy a T-shirt for £50, just because it has a logo on it, when for £15 you can get one that looks the same. I loved clothes and I loved being glamorous, but I just didn't get it. In her world, if it was in the sale, it was no good. Mad, eh? She would spend thousands on a single shopping trip, and she exercised loads, so she always was impeccably turned out.

I soon realized that Jude was unhappy in her marriage, and she was working out some issues with her self-esteem. She was always wanting me to meet up with her and some guy, who I would later realize was more than a friend. Justin gave me a hard time for going out with her. He said she was using me to cover up her affair. It didn't bother me, as it was her life to live, and she was a good friend to me in other ways.

Looking back on it now, I can see that there was a fair bit of manipulation going on. I can't believe I didn't see it at the time. Still, I enjoyed her company and as we grew closer, she became a great mentor to me. Some people called her the Ice Queen, but I saw her softer side. I understood her and I never judged her. She was her own person and could do as she wanted. Who am I to tell anyone how to live?

One evening, Justin and I went to our favorite restaurant, Shu, to have dinner and to talk to Alan, the owner, about our plans for the wedding reception. We knew him very well, as we were two of his most loyal customers. As Shu is located on the Lisburn Road, it is always crammed with the beautiful people of Belfast, and the atmosphere is buzzing.

Shu had become my go-to place. I often went there with my girlfriends or with clients. Every Christmas I would host a dinner for all my clients in the private dining room, and they always absolutely loved it. It was a way to express my appreciation of their loyalty, and it helped develop our relationships and generate more business. This was something Justin encouraged me to do, and, as I respect his business savvy, I listened. Every January, sales came flying in. People love to be appreciated.

I believe in building real relationships with my clients. I am always interested in their lives, and I have become friends with quite a few of them.

Justin would often say, "We need to buy that company."

I never wanted him to do that. By this time, I had moved into Justin's house and rented out my house out in Saintfield, which had been sitting vacant all this time. It didn't make sense having two places. He had purchased a lovely five-bedroom house on the Saintfield Road in Belfast, which was only about ten miles from my house. I liked having my independence and my own time away from him. My job was the part of my life that belonged to me. It was a separate world, and I wanted to keep it that way.

As our wedding day approached, Justin was finally ready to tell me exactly what he had planned for our honeymoon. As he proceeded to bring out the envelope containing our itinerary, I could see the excitement in his eyes. By now I knew how much he loves to travel in style, so I knew it was going to be five stars all the way.

"OK," he said, "are you ready? We'll start by flying first class to LA. The rest of the trip we'll fly business class. This is only for the trip out, to make it special."

I could hardly contain my excitement. Imagine flying British Airways in first class—that alone was a holiday to me. But that was only the beginning.

We would spend the night in Los Angeles before flying to Hawaii, where we would spend a week at the Four Seasons Resort Maui at Wailea.

From there we would fly to New Zealand, where we would rent a large camper van and travel through the North and South Island for two weeks.

Then we would fly to Sydney, where we would board a dive boat and spend three days diving at the Great Barrier Reef, finishing at Lizard Island. We'd be flown off the island on a six-seater to Port Douglas, where we would stay for a few nights.

We would then spend a few nights in Sydney, during which we would attend a show at the iconic Opera House, finishing with five days in Hong Kong.

I looked at him in disbelief. "How much is this going to cost?"

"Don't worry about that," he said. "This is something I have always wanted to do, and I can't think of anyone I would rather do this with."

I could barely take it all in. And yet, as excited and appreciative as I felt, I still failed to grasp exactly how amazing this trip would be.

We drank a lot of wine that evening, and I woke up the next morning with a hangover. My first thought was: *Did he really tell me we are flying first class on British Airways?*

I carefully rolled over, as my head was pounding. "Justin, did you tell me what I think you told me last night? Is this holiday really happening?"

"You better believe it," he said. "I have it all booked."

I could not believe it. I hugged him and thought, *I am so lucky. I have someone I am madly in love with, and he is kind, caring and romantic. We really have it all.* In my eyes, I was the happiest I had ever been.

On the morning of the wedding, I was at our home with Justin's daughter. She was so excited. I had helped her shop for a lovely outfit, and my friend Sonia was doing our hair and make-up. Justin stayed at his brother's house, so we would meet at the City Hall.

I had some champagne with my bridesmaids, and there was such a sense of excitement and fun that morning. I wore a long cream dress with a scooped back and some sparkles on it, and Sonia arranged my hair in an exquisite bridal updo. I hadn't spent too much time looking at lots of dresses. When I saw a dress I liked, I simply went for it. In my mind, it is about how you feel in the dress and not how anyone else thinks you should look.

I felt special that day. My sister was my witness, and my dad gave me away. This time, we didn't need to have that chat in the limo. He knew I was ready.

I felt like I was on top of the world. We all arrived at City Hall, and I went into a room where Justin would not see me. The Belfast City Hall is a magnificent building with Baroque Revival architecture. We got married in December, so it was festooned with Christmas decorations, making it appear even more spectacular.

I was very excited, but I was not as nervous as I had been at my first wedding. This was a more intimate affair in a small civil ceremony chamber, attended only by our immediate family. As I signed the book, I said to myself, *I am so happy to be with such a wonderful man.* I was looking forward to our wedding reception and seeing my family, friends, and colleagues.

After taking some photos, we left the City Hall and headed to our reception.

In the car, I turned to Justin and said, "If you ever have an affair, or if you hurt me in any way, I will leave you, so please don't do it. I so want a happy life with you."

He said, "I would never do that to you, babe. I love you so much."

"OK," I said. "I just had to say it."

Why did I say this? Why at that very moment? I sometimes think I am a witch. I have a sixth sense. I have instincts about people, and I can sense things before they happen. The only problem is, I never go with my gut feeling.

When we arrived at Shu for the wedding reception, the place was already filling up with our friends and family, and there was lots of love in the air. Everyone was so happy for us. The food was exquisite, and the music was great. We all danced up a storm, including my dad, who loved to dance every bit as much as I do.

At the end of the night, the realization dawned that we would be heading off for our six-week honeymoon the very next morning. I had mixed feelings about it. As excited as I was to be embarking upon this adventure, this would be the longest I had ever been apart from my family.

My dad came over to say goodbye to me. His shirt was soaked through from dancing, and he had tears in his eyes.

"Text and ring us whenever you can, OK?" He could barely get the words out. "Let us know how you are."

I nodded and hugged him. My sister, who rarely expresses any emotion, also appeared to be on the verge of tears, so I started to get quite choked up as well. I left the restaurant with a heavy heart. At the same time, it was nice to know how much my family was going to miss me. For the first time, I truly felt the depth of their love for me.

My second wedding - Shu Restaurant, Belfast

Honeymoon

The following morning, we set off on our honeymoon. As Justin had promised, we were flying to Los Angeles in first class on British Airways. I could hardly contain my excitement. We boarded the plane and settled into our stylish suites. Awaiting us were amenity kits containing luxury skincare products and everything else we might possibly need. They even supplied pyjamas.

Justin said, "It's a ten-hour flight. Get into your PJs and go to sleep."

"Sleep? No chance," I replied. "There's so much to do! Fine wine, fancy food, infinite movies, being treated like a princess. I want to savor every second of this flight."

He looked at me and said, "Stay up if you want, but you'd better be awake when we arrive. We're heading straight out for the evening. We have only one night in LA."

"Yes, of course!" I said, "I'll be good to go."

After the meal service, Justin dutifully converted the quilted seat into a flat bed and put on his sleep mask, even though it was daytime. Like an excited child, I stayed up for the entirety of the flight, watching movie after movie and basking in the VIP treatment.

After landing at LAX and clearing Customs and Immigration, we were whisked off to our hotel. As the sights and sounds of a sunny Los Angeles evening whizzed past the windows, I could barely keep my eyes open. As soon as we got to our hotel suite, I went straight to bed and crawled under the duvet. Justin was not impressed, but I could tell he was exhausted as well, though he wouldn't have admitted it. We both slept like babies and woke up feeling refreshed for our flight to Hawaii. I was glad we hadn't gone out the night before.

We arrived at the Four Seasons Resort Maui, a glamorous open-air waterfront resort on the crescent of Wailea Beach. Our room had an ocean view. I was overwhelmed all over again. It was like being in a fairytale. I was so in love with Justin, and we were about to spend the next six weeks together traveling the world.

I thought, *can life get any better than this? Thank you, God, for giving me so much.*

We spent the next five days indulging in all the niceties: culinary delights, massages at the beach, and champagne—lots of it. Justin had arranged for me to take a diving lesson. He loves to scuba dive, but ever since he punctured his lung in that carting accident, he is allowed only to snorkel. I slipped into the sea wearing all the scuba gear. Within minutes, I found myself gazing at turtles. It was magical.

We then flew to New Zealand, where we spent the next two weeks exploring the North and South Island in a camper van. At the end of a long day of driving, we would find a spot we liked and camp there for the night. We would have a barbecue on the beach, drink wine in the sunshine, and chill out.

Some nights, we would park at a vineyard. Of the many excellent vineyards we visited, one of my favorites was Cloudy Bay, whose Sauvignon Blanc is considered by many experts to be the best in the world. I brought six bottles around the world with me and back home.

We flew by helicopter up to the Franz Josef Glacier, rode a fly-by-wire glider, and soaked in the natural hot springs, which appear so idyllic but smell like rotten eggs.

New Zealand reminded me of Ireland in that it is very green and has lots of sheep. Their weather was like ours, even though it was their summertime when we visited. I treasured this part of our vacation. It was so relaxed and normal. As much as I loved living it up in fabulous hotels, I appreciated being able to kick back and let my hair down.

After this, we headed to Port Douglas, Australia. It was unbelievably hot, but we could not swim in the ocean as it was stinger season and the water was full of box jellyfish, which are the most venomous marine creatures.

We spent a few days in Sydney, Australia, before boarding the boat for a three-day excursion around the Great Barrier Reef. We shared the boat with about twenty other people, all of whom were experienced and passionate divers. When we arrived at the Cod Hole, I started to feel anxious about diving there, as it is in the middle of the ocean, and I have a fear of open water. As I didn't have even my first PADI certification, I was able to go down with the diver director. She held my hand, and I was delighted about this. I may not have attempted it otherwise.

Underwater, I encountered a different world—one filled with color, light, and tranquility. I was so stunned I had to remind myself to keep breathing. Iridescent fish swam around my face. I even saw sharks! Even though I had been told they would not attack us, they still scared me a bit.

In the evenings, we would have wine and food, and quite a few people would jump from the top of the boat into the sea. I was too scared to do so. They also participated in night dives, which I did not join. I was happiest diving in daylight. It was so hot, and I loved sitting on the top of the boat sunbathing after my dive. It was a lifechanging experience and one I will never forget.

For those three days, time seemed suspended, and yet it seemed to pass by in a flash. The boat docked at Lizard Island, where we waited for a small aircraft to fly us back to the mainland. On this island, lizards the size of Labradors ran around freely. I was so petrified I climbed up on the table to avoid them. I felt like I was in the movie *Jurassic Park*.

Our last stop was Hong Kong. It is a fascinating, diverse city where tradition and modernity live side by side. I was blown away to see how many designer shops can be packed into one city—I counted five Louis Vuitton stores in one day. I could not bear to see how cruelly the animals were treated in the markets. On the other hand, I loved visiting the zoo. I was incredibly excited to see pandas in real life. They are such awesome creatures. We spent a few evenings out and about, enjoying the food and the nightlife and soaking up the atmosphere. It was my first time to visit Southeast Asia, and I would love to return someday. I felt very fortunate to experience another culture.

We were staying in a fabulous hotel overlooking the bay, and the view of the harbor at night was mesmerizing.

On our last night, I said to Justin, "I just want to sit here with a drink and admire this view."

As much as I was looking forward to seeing my friends and my family again, I was sad that our six-week honeymoon was nearing its close. I had enjoyed every moment of our trip around the world, being in love and feeling as free as a bird.

Lovebug

As soon as we arrived back in Northern Ireland, I collected our dogs, Penny the Pom, and Ray the Saint Bernard. By now, they probably had forgotten who we were. It felt like we had been away forever. It was wonderful to reunite with my family and friends and get back to my routine. I loved my life at home.

We resumed living at Justin's house, and I threw myself back into work. I was busy looking after some major blue chip companies. My role was to manage the customers and negotiate with the companies from whom we were outsourcing a lot of our print. It was very enjoyable, as the company trusted me and granted me a lot of autonomy. I received my new company car—a silver Mercedes SLK hard-top convertible, which I loved. Having this car made me feel that my hard work was appreciated.

When we had been married for a year, we began looking for a new home. Justin wanted to be closer to his workplace and his kids, so we settled on a beautiful, detached home on the coast of County Down near Sketrick Island. It had stables, and I intended to buy a horse for myself and for Justin's daughter. She's an animal lover who also loves to ride.

During our last viewing of the new house, I was approached by a fluffy Collie dog, who licked my hands and clearly wanted some attention. He had the most amazing, happy face. I instantly loved him. A lady came walking up behind him.

"What's his name?" I asked her.

"Bertie," she said. "If you know anyone who wants him, they can have him. Otherwise, he will be going to the pound, as I don't want him anymore."

"What?" I was horrified. "How can you give this gorgeous creature away?"

"I got him as a guard dog," she said, as if that explained everything.

"Right, that's it. We are keeping him," I said.

"Yes, we are," Justin said. "He will be a great friend for Ray."

It's sad that some people don't appreciate that a dog is a true friend. To me, Bertie looked like a little lovebug, so I was happy we could rescue him. Now we were the proud owners of three dogs. It was perfect, as our new house had an enormous garden and outbuildings right on the back of the lough. The dogs would have plenty of room to run around and we would be able to take them on beautiful walks.

Six months later, we moved into our new home. I loved it. We were far from the city now, so it wasn't as easy to go out there in the evenings, and I had a longer commute to work, which meant an earlier start for me. I easily adjusted to these changes, as I loved the countryside and the local country pubs.

It seemed that Justin was always away, whether traveling for work, skiing or attending a Grand Prix. This was fine with me, as I believe we should all live our lives and retain our interests regardless of whether we are in a relationship. I didn't expect Justin to give up the things he loved or to spend all his time with me.

I took the opportunity to spend time with my friends. We would often go on weekend trips to Dublin for shopping and nights out. I still loved the buzz and excitement of Dublin City just as much as I always had. For me, it was like going to another planet. It was so different from Belfast, and I was always drawn to it.

I once asked Justin, "Can we not move to Dublin? You could open a branch there."

"No," he said, "it's too expensive." With that, he shut me down.

I was enjoying married life, and I really loved my relationship with Justin's kids. We genuinely cared for each other, and I counted myself fortunate to have a perfect readymade family.

My Bertie – Holywood

A Day at the Palace

My dad was being awarded an MBE (Member of the Order of the British Empire) for his work advocating for anti-sectarianism in the workplace. My dad had left his job at British Telecom to establish an organization called Counteract, which was an offshoot of the trade unions involved with BT. He was passionate about helping others and working to resolve the divide between Catholics and Protestants in the workplace. Yet he was a modest man, without an ounce of entitlement. In fact, I had to convince him to accept the MBE. I felt he truly deserved this recognition, having put himself on the line on many occasions, and I was delighted that he would be receiving this very prestigious honor.

The Investiture ceremony takes place at Buckingham Palace every year, and the Queen or another member of the Royal Family presents the awards. This particular year, the awards would be presented by the Queen herself. As neither my sister nor my brother was free to attend, Justin and I proposed that we bring my mum to London, so that the three of us could accompany my father to the ceremony. Though my mum rarely travels, she loved the idea and agreed to come along. Justin reserved rooms at a lovely hotel and arranged for us to have dinner at a famous restaurant to mark the occasion.

I was excited to have the opportunity to visit Buckingham Palace. I bought a floaty pink outfit and a pink matching hat to wear. While I am not a Royalist, I respect Queen Elizabeth II as an individual. I feel she has borne a great deal of responsibility since she was very young and has always undertaken her duties with great dedication and enthusiasm.

The sun was shining that day in London, as we stood before the iconic, wrought-iron gates adorned with the Royal Coat of Arms. It felt somewhat unreal to say our names and be allowed to enter the palace. As we walked along the corridors flanked by the Queen's Guards in their sharp red tunics and bearskin hats, I thought, *Gosh, how do they remain so poised and so immaculate?* The atmosphere felt hallowed. We took our seats near the front of the ceremonial hall, while my dad remained at the back of the hall with the other honorees.

Justin turned to me and said, "Isn't it great to be part of the British Empire?"

I laughed. Unlike me, Justin is so British. I am very moderate in my views. While I am proud that Northern Ireland is part of the United Kingdom, I always view myself as Irish.

A hush came over the room as the Queen emerged, and the ceremony commenced. As I watched my father approach the Queen, I was bursting with pride. The Queen shook his hand and briefly spoke with him about his work before presenting him with the award. It was a moment I will never forget.

My dad was greatly loved and respected by everyone who knew him. He had a magnetic personality and a balanced outlook on life. He was never one to judge and accepted everyone at face value. He would often say, "Denise, no matter how badly a person has betrayed you, always kill them with kindness."

While this is valuable advice, I must admit, being a hothead like my mum, I find it tough to carry out. We all had a superb night out afterwards and returned home the next day with glorious memories of having been at Buckingham Palace with the Queen.

Descent

I began noticing some subtle changes in Justin's behavior. He was often unavailable when I phoned, and he seemed somewhat distant at times. I kept telling myself to stop imagining the worst. He was a busy man.

And yet, I couldn't shake the feeling that something was off. The truth was, although I could explain away every odd little thing he did, my sense of foreboding didn't originate in those odd little things; it came from somewhere deep within me. I could feel it in my gut, inside my bones. As I said, I'm intuitive—a witch.

One evening, Justin's cellphone rang while he was out of the room. I called out to him: "Your phone is ringing!"

I listened. No response. His phone was still ringing, so I answered it, thinking it might be one of our friends and I would just chat to them until Justin came back. The caller immediately hung up. Back then, cellphones simply showed you the number that had called you and not the caller's name. I wondered who it was.

Right then, Justin entered the room. "Why did you answer that?" he asked sharply.

"You weren't here," I said. "I just thought—"

My voice trailed off when I saw the horrified look on his face. Even though I had been feeling apprehensive lately, I hadn't answered the call out of nosiness. But the way he was acting now made my paranoia resurface.

"They hung up as soon as I picked up," I said. "Don't you think that's weird?"

He didn't answer.

"Who do you think it was?" I asked.

"How would I know?" he said. "They might ring back."

I didn't know what else to say, so I let it slide.

Life carried on for a while. Then, one night, it happened again. Another call came through when Justin's phone was left unattended. It rang and rang and didn't go to voicemail. I picked up.

Another hang-up.

"What are you doing?" Justin said. "Why are you torturing yourself over nothing? You've got to stop."

I dropped it, but now my radar was up. I knew he had been unfaithful in past relationships, and I wondered if he was up to his old tricks again.

I decided to take to my mum and my sister to London for the day to do some shopping. Flights were so cheap, and I thought it would be a nice thing for the three of us to do together. It was an early start for my mum, so she became quite tired halfway through the trip, but I made sure both she and my sister had an exciting and memorable day.

At the same time, I was finding it hard to relax and enjoy myself, as I couldn't get hold of Justin. I rang him throughout the day, but he didn't answer any of my calls, and he never phoned or texted back. As the hours wore on, I began to worry myself sick. My fear, that something awful had happened to him, dampened what should have been a fun day out in London.

Finally, as we boarded our flight home, Justin phoned me. I was incredibly relieved to hear his voice, but I was annoyed that it had taken him all day to get back to me. He said he had been in a business meeting all morning and had gone straight to a lunch that had carried on much longer than expected. I didn't believe him. I wondered what was really going on.

A few weeks later, we were down at the summer house in Enniskillen when he received a call from a woman. She was someone he knew from the motor trade. When he answered, I could hear her inviting him out for drinks. The whole thing was very awkward, and I went mad.

"Why would a single girl ring you on a Sunday and ask you to go out drinking?"

He made up another bullshit story, but I wasn't falling for it.

First thing on Monday morning, I phoned this girl and asked her why she felt she could ring up a married man on a Sunday and ask him out for drinks. She said she had meant to call another friend, who also happened to be named Justin, and had simply phoned the wrong Justin.

"I don't believe you," I told her. "Never ring my husband again."

I started to feel insecure about our marriage. Had I made the right decision in marrying him? Could I trust him? Why was I even in this position? Why should I have to phone up some woman and question her about ringing my husband? With these questions swirling in my mind, I felt so sad and scared. I didn't know what to do. All I knew was that I didn't want to feel like this all the time, so I decided to move past it and let it go.

By now, Justin was always either working late or away on a business trip or a holiday. I kept myself busy with work, going to the gym, and spending time with my friends, my family, and my dogs. I started seeing more of my friend Nuala. We had known each other for a few years by then. We would often meet for dinner after work. Nuala was a great girl. She was single, and she had been hurt by many of the men in her life. I often confided in her about my feelings, and she really understood what I was going through.

One evening, Justin came home from work and said, "Let's go to Marbella with Sonia and Bernard."

"Yeah, that would be great," I said.

Sonia is a great friend of mine, and her partner, Bernard, is a real country guy. They both love horses. They are into eventing and hunting, so they belong to the horsey world, but they also love to get away and have fun.

A week later, the four of us heading to Marbella for the weekend. We had a marvelous time sunbathing, dining out, and drinking way too much. We went out shopping in Puerto Banús, and I remember looking at a Christian Dior handbag that cost a thousand euros. I said to Sonia, "Isn't this nice? But wow—it's pretty expensive!"

We left the shop and just as we arrived at the bar, Justin said that Bernard had a headache, so they were going to the pharmacy to get some ibuprofen. Sonia and I found a table and ordered a couple of gin and tonics. After some time, the guys appeared, and Justin presented me with the Dior bag. I was floored.

"Why did you buy this for me?" I asked Justin. "It's not that I don't appreciate the gesture, but I wasn't in love with it or anything. And it's way too expensive."

"I wanted to surprise you," he said.

I was thrilled, and yet I thought it was a strange thing for him to do. When I would spend €300 on a bag, Justin always said it was excessive, even though he had introduced me to designer bags in the first place.

"Flip, Denise, that's a lot of money," Sonia said.

"I know," I replied, "and for a bag I wasn't even mad about!"

Soon after this, Justin and I spent a weekend in Paris. The highlight of our trip was the dinner show at the Moulin Rouge, which was simply spectacular. I had always wanted to see it. As we walked hand in hand through the picturesque streets of this city of exceptional style, beauty, and romance, Justin seemed to be in a lovey-dovey mood. And yet, I still had the underlying feeling that something was not quite right.

Upon returning home, we learned that Justin's dad had been involved in a serious accident on the farm and was in critical condition. We rushed straight to the hospital, where he lay in a coma. We both were utterly distraught.

I loved Justin's dad. He was a true character, with a large belly and only a few front teeth, so I always called him the Toothless Wonder. He was larger than life, in terms of his physical presence as well as his personality. I went to the hospital many times to visit him. He had sustained such grave injuries that the doctors had to amputate his legs. During this time, Justin continued to travel a lot for work. I sensed that he was trying to brace himself for what was coming next.

Justin's dad never regained consciousness. When he passed away, Justin was heartbroken. I really felt for him. He seemed to withdraw even further into himself, and I had no idea how to reach him. Many people attended the funeral.

I remember saying to Justin, "I know you are so proud of your dad. Speak of him often, in memory of his remarkable life."

Not long afterwards, our Saint Bernard died of a tumor. Large dogs tend to have shorter life spans, due to their large limbs. It was a terribly sad autumn. Justin immersed himself in his work and often went away on business trips. Even when he was at home, he seemed a million miles away. I knew that when a person is grieving, they need to heal in their own way and its best not to crowd them. I tried to be there for him while allowing him the space to heal.

Christmas

The holidays were approaching. We decided we would spend Christmas at home and then set off on Boxing Day for a three-week holiday in South Africa. I had never been there before, and I really looked forward to it. In the time leading up to our trip, Justin frequently traveled for work. I was extremely busy at work, and I was also occupied with decorating our new home. I was drowning in paint, curtain and carpet samples and dreaming about our amazing holiday.

I said to Justin, "Let's cook Christmas dinner in our new home for my family and your kids."

"Yes," he said. "What a great idea."

I set about planning a beautiful day for everyone. I wanted to do something special for Justin, as I really appreciated how well he treated me. I decided to spend my November commission on a Cartier watch for him. It cost around £3,000. I could hardly wait to give it to him on Christmas Day.

One sunny Friday morning, I was driving up to Downpatrick to see one of my customers. It was a Korean company, and the client always called me Dennis. She had phoned me earlier and said, "Dennis, are you coming? I have a big order for you."

I had jumped into my little convertible with the top down and was happily speeding along, wind blowing my hair, music blasting. In a week, we would be setting off for our South African adventure. I was as happy as a child. Even though it was December, the sun was shining. It felt like a spring day, and I was beaming with happiness. On impulse, I phoned Justin.

"I'm just calling to tell you how happy I am and how much I love you," I said. "We have everything we could ever want. I love our new home, and I'm so excited to go to South Africa with you."

There was silence.

"Hello?" I said.

"Why are you saying all this?"

"Why not? I'm so happy. Everything's perfect."

"Yes, yes. Of course," he said. "I just hope you haven't gotten me anything too extravagant for Christmas."

My heart sank, but I laughed airily. "That's for me to know and for you to find out," I said lightly.

I came off the phone feeling like my joy had been flattened by a steamroller. Fear gripped me. Why wasn't he as happy as I was? He had sounded weirdly guilty. I reminded myself that whenever he wasn't traveling, he was always home at night. He never stayed out late, so he could not possibly be cheating on me. I thought he must still be mourning the loss of his father.

In the week leading up to Christmas, I was juggling work with planning all the Christmas festivities, putting up decorations, buying presents for everyone, and packing for the three-week holiday. Justin's daughter helped me with the meal preparations and organizing the table for Christmas Day. A few days before Christmas, Justin had to go to Dublin at short notice. Something work-related, he said. I was so busy that I didn't think much about it.

On Saturday morning, I needed to pick up a lot of shopping for the Christmas dinner. As I wouldn't be able to fit everything inside my car, I decided to take Justin's Range Rover, but I couldn't find the keys anywhere. I kept phoning Justin to ask where they were, but I couldn't reach him. He phoned me back four hours later. By that stage, I was climbing the walls, as you can imagine. My head was all over the place.

By now, I was sure he was up to something, but I couldn't pin him down. He was too devious. He said he had been stuck in meetings. Who has meetings on the Saturday before Christmas? Deep down, I knew was being played, but I wanted to believe in him—in us. I told myself I was being paranoid, that it was all in my mind. I simply hoped for the best.

When he finally came home, he was exhausted. He slept through most of Christmas Day.

"Why is he so tired?" my mum asked me.

"He has had a busy time recently. With us going away soon, he has had lots to do."

"This is just not like him," she said.

Cape Town

After spending a lovely Christmas with my family and Justin's kids, we were heading off to South Africa. We would fly into Cape Town, travel along the Garden Route, and then spend three days on safari in Kruger National Park. I was so excited. We flew out in business class on British Airways.

As we lounged in our suites sipping champagne, I asked Justin, "Why were you so tired on Christmas Day?"

"I have a lot going on at work," he said. "I had to wrap up some things before we went away."

"Both your daughter and I put in a lot of time and effort to make it a really special Christmas."

"And I appreciate it. But you shouldn't have spent so much money on my present," he said, changing the subject. "It was a little over the top."

"I gave you the watch because I wanted to," I said. "When something is given to you with love, you should accept it."

"OK," he said. "I'm going to get some sleep."

"Fine," I said. "I am going to have a lovely drink and enjoy the movies."

There is something so special about flying business class. To me, it is part of the holiday. The anticipation of the trip, while travelling in comfort and style, is absolutely thrilling. I could have pinched myself every time.

When we arrived in Cape Town, we checked in at The Twelve Apostles, a plush oceanfront hotel named after the mountain range that towers above it. We would be staying there for three nights. Our bed was on a platform with double doors that opened out onto the sea. We could hear the waves crashing against the shore. I could have sat there all day watching the ocean. It was an absolute dream.

The next morning after breakfast, Justin said, "I need to collect the rental car. Why don't you stay here? You can relax and sunbathe by the pool."

That sounded lovely to me, as it was a scorching day, and the pool was awesome. I spent the rest of the morning lounging beside the pool, then had lunch on my own. As the afternoon wore on, I began to wonder what was taking Justin so long.

When he finally returned, I asked him, "Where did you go for the car?"

"Back to Ireland," he said. He laughed. "Nah, it just took longer than expected."

I had a clear notion that he had been talking on the phone with another woman. It was so specific that I had to question myself for thinking of it. Of all the things he could have been doing, why did I believe he was speaking on the phone to someone? But I couldn't shake the feeling. Doubt and suspicion filled my mind, and I was dying to get hold of his phone and look through his recent calls. I held back from doing so. Although I had the right to know what was really going on, I did not feel right about invading his privacy.

The next day, we visited Robben Island, where Nelson Mandela was detained for eighteen of the twenty-seven years he was held as a political prisoner. The tour was conducted by another former inmate, who shared his experience of and insight into what had taken place there. I was able to sit in the cell that held Nelson Mandela. This whole experience was very moving.

We then headed off in our rental car to Table Mountain and began our journey along the Garden Route. Along the way, we stayed at various well-appointed hotels, some by the sea, others in the forest, each having its own exquisite brand of charm. We met fascinating people and visited picturesque vineyards. My favorite might have been Stellenbosch, not only for its wine, but also for the individuality of the town. It was as if a small piece of Europe had been transplanted to South Africa.

Stellenbosch is home to many superb restaurants and boutiques, including diamond stores. Justin was keen to buy me a dazzling diamond bangle. As enchanting as it was, I declined his offer, as I felt that we had spent quite enough money already. I was happy buying African trinkets. By this stage, we had almost filled up an extra suitcase. I was having an amazing time, and I kept thinking how happy I was.

We continued to make our way along the Garden Route. We arrived in Knysna, a true natural wonderland renowned for its spectacular lagoon. As we checked into our sumptuous hotel, the midday heat was oppressive. We had travelled a fair bit that day.

I said to Justin, "Let's spend the afternoon just relaxing by the pool."

We settled in by the pool and ordered some lunch and a bottle of rosé. You can't beat chilled rosé at lunchtime in the sun—it simply tastes so much better than white, and it's much more refreshing. I was looking forward to spending a gorgeous day in this tranquil setting. I felt so relaxed. Everything was perfect.

"Let's just stay right here all day," I said. "We can have dinner here tonight."

"Yeah, great," Justin said. "I'll just run up to the room to use the bathroom and get changed."

"OK," I said, reclining on the lounger.

As the sun warmed my body, I switched off all my thoughts about work and everything else that was going on in my life. I closed my eyes and listened to the birds sing. I felt so blissful. Our lunch arrived. I began to wonder what was taking Justin so long. I decided to go up and see what was keeping him. As I approached our room, I decided I would enter quietly. I wanted to see exactly what he was doing.

In the room, he was nowhere to be found. Then, I noticed that the bathroom door was ajar. I could see him perched on the edge of the bathtub, texting. I didn't make a sound. As he gazed at his phone with total concentration, he was so immersed in what he was doing that he didn't notice me tiptoeing into the bathroom. As soon as I was close enough, I snatched his phone out of his hands.

He almost jumped out of his skin. "What are you doing?"

"No," I said, "what are *you* doing? I've been sitting out there for ages on my own."

My body shook uncontrollably as I began to read the message out loud. "Hi, darling, from so many thousand miles away, I am getting closer to you—"

My voice cracked as I started to cry, but I kept reading through my tears. "It won't be long until I see you. I miss you so much. What the fuck?"

I could feel my heart shattering into tiny pieces as I looked at him. For the first time in a long time, he met my gaze. All the blood had drained out of his face. He looked like a ghost. His expression chilled me to the bone—an innocent man wouldn't be looking at me like this.

I stared into his eyes for a moment and then looked back down at the screen. Phones were different then. As he had still been composing the message, I couldn't tell who its intended recipient was. All I knew was that I wasn't crazy. My paranoia, intuition—whatever you wanted to call it—had been right all along. Something about the wording of the message made me think it was not someone from home. I felt it was a person somewhere else in the world.

"What the fuck is going on?" I demanded. "Justin, for once, I am begging you—just give me a straight answer."

"Nothing. I was texting my daughter," he said.

"I know that was not for her. Stop making an idiot out of me. *Who is she?*"

"Look, it's not what you think."

"Yeah, yeah," I said. "I'm not an idiot. I want to go home now. I am not spending another week in this beautiful place with a liar. You better tell me the truth before I go home and tell everyone."

Just then, I began to grasp the enormity of his betrayal. How long had this been going on behind my back? The shock, anger and sadness hit me all at once. I didn't know what to do.

I phoned my dad and told him everything. He was gutted on my behalf. "You don't know any of the details," he said. "Maybe you should stay there until the end of the holiday and try to find out everything. Get him to come clean. What's the point in coming back early? Just enjoy yourself the best you can."

"OK, I will do that," I said.

How was I going to get through this holiday? I felt like Justin had stabbed me in the heart. I had always known he'd been unfaithful in past relationships, but I had never thought he would do this to me. Why had he pushed so hard for marriage, only to betray me?

We stayed in the room arguing and crying from two in the afternoon until after midnight. I was so hungry, but I couldn't force myself to eat. I went to sleep that night with his phone under my pillow, hoping the other woman would send a text. I needed to know who she was.

Safari

I held onto Justin's phone for the rest of the holiday, in the hopes that she would make contact, but she never did. That first night, I had phoned one of Justin's friends. I found out later that he had warned the other woman that I had found out about the affair. I kept begging Justin to tell me who she was. At the very least, I deserved to know the truth.

"Why won't you tell me?" I asked him. "Is it someone I know? Please don't tell me it's someone at home who's been laughing at me the whole time."

"Of course it's not," he would say. "Please, Denise. It's nothing."

He tortured my mind for the rest of the holiday. I was a mess. I felt so betrayed and so hurt. I kept remembering all the times I had felt that something was going on, and all the times he had denied it. Everything was starting to make sense.

As we approached the end of the holiday, we flew out of Port Elizabeth on a small aircraft. We would be spending the last four days of the holiday on safari. I had so looked forward to this part of the vacation. Now, a cloud of sadness hovered over me. In such a short time, my life had completely unraveled.

I felt so lost, so destroyed. My mind was spinning. *What did I do to deserve this? All I ever did was love him. Did I love him too much? I feel ugly. I feel worthless. Why aren't I enough for him? What does he need that I can't give him? Did he ever really love me?*

Against the backdrop of the magnificent safari park, I kept asking him, "What's really going on? Please, Justin, just tell me."

He wouldn't tell me the truth. It was amazing to be on safari, surrounded by all the animals I love. But I felt broken.

I kept thinking, *What happens after this? What will I do when I get home?*

One morning, I awoke to the sound of monkeys screaming. They were warning all the other monkeys that lions were nearby. It was such an awesome sound, and it made me think, *That is how I feel. I am warning myself of what lies ahead.* I was screaming inside.

When our plane touched down in Belfast, I turned to Justin and said, "Now I will find out exactly what has been going on."

I knew there was a lot more to this than he was letting on, and I was determined to get to the bottom of it.

Surfacing

The following day, I went to Justin's office and combed through his email messages until I found what I was looking for—incontestable evidence that he was having an extramarital affair. Learning the truth was satisfying and sickening at the same time. It was incredibly painful to know beyond a doubt that Justin had been betraying me and lying to me for months on end. The only relief came from finally having proof that this wasn't all in my head, as he had led me to believe for so long.

The email correspondence provided a detailed chronicle of how it all had unfolded. He had met this woman at the Hungarian Grand Prix, and they had slept together that very night. This marked the beginning of their affair. At that point, we had been married for a year and a half.

He had flown her to various destinations to meet him whenever he was traveling for business or other purposes. In one of the email messages, he had said: *I love my wife, but I am in love with you.* Reading those words was sheer agony for me.

I found photos of the two of them at the Guinness Brewery in Dublin at Christmas, when I was at home cooking dinner for our families. In the pictures, he is wearing his wedding ring on a different finger. When I saw this, my pain escalated to a new level. It tore right through my heart and soul.

"Who is this whore?" I screamed, whacking him over the head with my handbag.

I was so enraged I could barely see. He kept his head down as I stormed out of his office, shouting and screaming. I was hysterical.

Later, his accountant phoned me. She said, "I'm so sorry, Denise, but I knew. I have known for some time. I found some information, but I couldn't bring myself to tell you. If you like, you can come and get it tomorrow."

I went to see her the following day. She gave me everything she had collected, and this helped me to fill in more of the blanks.

This may sound strange, but from the day he had started the affair, I knew it in my heart. I felt it in my gut. To this day, I cannot understand why I didn't follow up on my instincts. Why didn't I push a little harder and investigate further? Perhaps I hadn't really wanted to know. Now I knew, and I had a choice to make.

If this had been a one-night stand or a short-term fling, I might have been able to forgive him. But this had carried on for a long time. They must have formed an emotional connection as well.

As I drove my car back to the house that day, I could hardly see the road in front of me. I was crying hysterically and couldn't stop. My heart felt like it was being ripped out of my chest. The pain was unbearable. I imagined driving my car into the hedges and hoping I would never wake up.

Soon after I arrived at the house, my parents came over. I was so devastated I could barely speak. I stood there, in our new home, surrounded by the boxes I hadn't yet unpacked. I would likely be moving out before I had really moved in.

My dad hugged me and said, "I am so sorry. This is simply awful."

Justin arrived. He stood by the kitchen door with his head down.

My mum said, "Justin, can I just ask you why?"

"I felt like Denise didn't love me enough," he replied.

Hearing those words come out of his mouth made my blood boil. I ran over and started blindly kicking and punching him. "How can you say that? How can you think you can do what you did, and blame it on *me*? No one could have loved you more than I do! No one!" I realized I was screaming.

"Denise, stop," my mum said, pulling me away.

I wanted to hurt Justin as much as he had hurt me, but I didn't know how. I knew that the woman lived with her partner in Budapest, so I contacted them both and informed her partner about the affair.

When Justin found out what I had done, he was annoyed with me, but I didn't care. I was filled with anger and despair, and pain unlike anything I had ever experienced. Although I had threatened to go over and knock ten lamps out of her, I knew this wouldn't help me to heal. I finally told Justin that unless he moved out of the house, I could not be held responsible for what I might do.

The evening he left, all my closest girlfriends braved intense thunderstorms to come down and stay with me. My best friend, Andrea, drove all the way from Antrim through merciless, hammering rain. At times like these, your real friends come through for you.

That evening was like a funeral wake, but one where the corpse is still walking around. I had been drinking wine all day, and I felt like I was having an out-of-body experience. The lounge was covered in souvenirs from our South African holiday, and I kept looking at them and crying.

I was inconsolable. I hated myself. Why would anyone want to hurt me so badly when all I had done was love them? Could I ever learn to love again? How was I supposed to carry on?

The following week was one of the most hellish times in my life. I refused to let Justin back into the house, though I missed him terribly. It is the weirdest feeling to love and hate a person at the same time.

After a few weeks, I had to let Justin come back to the house. That was when I told him I was moving out. He begged me to give him another chance. He said he loved me and was sorry for what he had done. He had ended his relationship with the other woman and was committed to making things work with me.

I told him I couldn't stay with him, as I would never be able to trust him again. I wished that none of this had ever happened, but there was no way to turn back the clock. The damage had been done.

My friend Kathy took me to Edinburgh for the weekend, just so I could get away from it all for a few days. We went shopping, and I remember spending £1,000 on clothes I didn't really want. I just wanted something to numb the pain. On the Saturday evening we went to the Opal Rooms, and the England Rugby team were there that evening, but I couldn't get excited. I felt dead inside.

Kathy did her best to cheer me up, but I was in such a dark place. On my way to the restroom, I walked past a group of guys and thought I heard them say, *Look at that woman. She's so fat and ugly.*

Of course, those were my demons speaking. Justin's affair had made me feel utterly worthless. I realized I had internalized his actions to the point where, on some level, I blamed myself for his behavior. I truly believed that what he had done meant that I wasn't enough.

When I came back to the table, I told Kathy what I had just experienced.

She said, "You need to go and see a therapist. You are angry, and rightly so."

When we got back to the hotel; I could not stop crying. I was at rock bottom, and I had no idea how to make things better.

Rebirth

When I returned from Edinburgh, I began setting up my new life. I sought legal advice from a solicitor. I wanted to move out of the house, but he advised against doing so. As I didn't want to keep on living there, the solicitor drew up some paperwork, which granted me the latitude to move out for six months and rent my own place while coming to my final decision. Justin was not too thrilled about this arrangement, but he had to accept the terms. After all, he had created the situation that had led us here.

    I rented a beautiful little cottage in Cultra, an exclusive residential neighborhood near Holywood, a town in the metropolitan area of Belfast in County Down. I had always wanted to live there, as it is near the sea and close to the city. It seemed like a good place in which to get my head together and figure out how to move forward with my life.

    I moved all my belongings out of our house. It was incredibly painful, but I got through it. Somehow, I found my inner strength and managed to push myself through every agonizing moment of this ordeal. I told Justin I would be keeping Bertie, our Collie, and Penny, my little Pomeranian.

The three of us moved out to the cottage, which had a beautiful garden and a fabulous open fire. It was a great little retreat, and a safe space where I could begin the healing process. On most days, I would arrive home from work to find flowers, teddy bears or other gifts waiting for me. I ignored these empty gestures. I still wanted to kill him.

I could not forgive Justin for what he had done to me. Eighteen months into our marriage—a marriage *he* had pushed for—he had become sexually and emotionally involved with another person. When questioned, he had covered up his infidelity by lying to me and gaslighting me. The gaslighting was almost as hard to forgive as the affair itself. It's bad enough to lie to a person's face; making them question their own sense of reality, in the effort to cover your own ass, is truly amoral.

My rage was a blessing. It kept me strong. Whenever I began to miss him, I remembered how seeing and reading their photos and email messages had hurt me deep inside. I knew too much about the affair, and there was no way for me to get past it. I had to stay away and try to keep moving forward without him. I had given up the person I loved and the lifestyle and security he provided, but I valued myself more than all those things combined. I knew I deserved better.

I was starting over at the age of thirty-four. I had a great job, amazing friends, a good heart, and a lot of love to give. I believed I would eventually meet someone who was perfect for me. I enjoyed living at the cottage. I was close to the beach, so I walked the dogs there every evening and most mornings, as I was often up before seven. I couldn't sleep, and I didn't have much appetite. I kept losing weight.

On nights out, I always went into Belfast city. I never socialized in the village. On so many evenings, I would come back to the cottage and cry my eyes out. I still felt destroyed by what had happened. I hated myself, and I hated people talking about me. I felt as if the whole world thought I was a joke. My mind was always filled with these destructive thoughts. The demons just wouldn't shut up.

I went to Marbella with an estate agent and paid a deposit of £5,000 towards an apartment. I thought if I moved away, I could make a fresh start. Perhaps I could sell real estate there. I never went ahead with the move, and I lost my deposit. I realized I wasn't ready to leave home and move there. I had just been kidding myself. Anyway, there was no point in running away from the pain. No matter where I went, it would follow me.

I decided to go to therapy, as Kathy had suggested. I was still holding on to so much anger, and my mind was in constant turmoil. Being betrayed and deceived by someone I loved had caused me to doubt everything else I thought I knew, including myself and my thoughts. It was time I got some help.

A good friend recommended her own therapist, Clare. Her office was warm and cozy, filled with beautiful cushions in jewel tones. As soon as I walked in, I began to feel relaxed and at ease. Clare has curly blond hair and a warm and friendly face. Feeling soothed by her soft vocal tones and caring, compassionate approach, I started to cry uncontrollably.

She came over and hugged me, saying, "It's all going to be OK."

Once I had calmed down again, she asked me to describe my relationship with my mother.

"Why?" I asked.

"Just tell me a bit about her."

"OK," I said.

Clare listened intently as I described the relationship dynamic I have with my mum. When I had finished, she said, "Keep going."

I said, "I am here to talk about Justin."

"I know," she said, "but let's leave that for the moment and talk about your mum."

This was when I started to understand why I had made the choices I made. We learn about love from our parents, and because of the way my mother had treated me, I mistook all controlling and abusive relationships for love. I thought love was all about trying to get someone to love you, just as I had always tried to get my mum to love me.

Clare said, "This is what we need to work on first."

This was a huge revelation, but it was only the beginning. I still couldn't see my life clearly. I could see it a little.

I began seeing Clare every week, and each time we talked I discovered something new about myself.

Whenever I would tell her about a man I met, she would ask me, "Is he emotionally available?"

I always said, "I don't know."

This was a new concept for me, and I couldn't yet grasp what it really meant.

Clare helped me to gain a better understanding of myself and my relationships. I would advise anyone who is coming out of a relationship or going through any kind of transition to talk things over with a therapist. We can all benefit from some professional guidance as we work on developing ourselves.

During the six-month grace period I had been granted for thinking things over, Justin persisted in trying to get me to come back to him. He can be very persuasive and it is hard to refuse him, but I did. Even though he had ended his affair, I couldn't go back to him. Deep down, I knew he would do it to me again and again. The last months had been pure hell. I didn't want to live like that. He had destroyed my trust. If I was going to learn how to trust again, it would have to be with someone else.

When the six months were up, I told him all I wanted was half of the value of our house. I wanted to be able to take out a mortgage on a new home, as I had sold mine when I moved into his place.

Justin said, "Once you take your half of the house, it's really over between us."

He was manipulating the narrative to make me responsible for breaking up our relationship, even though it had been his choices and his actions that had broken us up. *It was over between us once you started regularly fucking someone else and lying to me,* I thought.

I just said, "I know. I loved you so much, and I still do, but I can never trust you again."

If I received my half of the house value, I had no interest in claiming alimony or getting anything else from Justin. Many people said I was stupid for not having taken him to the cleaners, but I stand by my decision. During our time together, Justin had treated me to the finer things in life. We had travelled to all kinds of fascinating places, and I felt I had learned a lot from him. I wanted to cut my losses and move on.

I understand that many women, especially those who have married young, may have made sacrifices in their education or their career to raise a family. They may still be raising their children, so for them it is necessary to claim alimony and child support. We didn't have children, and I had continued working during our marriage. I had a good job, so I would be fine.

I didn't want to claim financial support to punish Justin for having been unfaithful to me. Even though he had hurt me more than I can express, I wanted to get on with my life. I knew that dragging this through the court system and fighting about money would only keep the pain alive and stop me from moving on.

I remember telling Justin, "Someday I will be happy and find someone who will not do this to me. You will most likely never be happy."

Right next door to the cottage I was renting was a lovely Georgian house that had been split into two houses. One of them had been put up for sale. I took out a mortgage on it. When I told my dad, he was not happy.

He said, "You are paying a lot of money for half a house. It's very old and will need constant upkeep. It will be a lot of work."

I considered this, but then I followed my heart and stuck with my decision. I love old properties with a lot of character, so this house was perfect in my eyes. It had a garden for the dogs and was right beside the sea.

I was still seeing Clare every week, and she was helping me to deal with the pain I was experiencing in the aftermath of Justin's affair and our divorce. I was really struggling to love—or even to like—myself. Having been married twice at the age thirty-four was not exactly the future I would have envisioned for myself. I needed to start looking at my life and making different choices.

Clare helped me to identify the sources of my insecurities, which helped me understand why I was making certain decisions and falling for certain people. I learned that my relationship dynamic with my mother had instilled in me a deep longing for affection, and this has made me particularly susceptible to love bombing—a manipulation tactic all the great loves of my life have deployed in one form or another.

Whether it was conscious or unconscious on their part, each of them had showered me with gifts and attention, to influence my emotions and ultimately try to control me. I always took this behavior at face value: *He must really like me and care about me. He is generous and kind. He is just the type who comes on strong.*

Even once I was made aware of my destructive patterns of thought and behavior, it took a long time for me to change them, as they had been with me since childhood and had become deeply ingrained.

I was proud of myself for having had the courage to leave my marriages when they stopped being healthy for me, but I still harbored a lot of negative emotions from the breakups, and from the relationships themselves. The guilt and shame that you experience when you leave someone are even more intense when you leave the type of person who feels they deserve your love, no matter what. On top of this, I was still dealing with the long-term psychological effects of being in intimate relationships with controlling people. It was hard for me to see the good in myself, and I often felt like I was in a weird, self-destructive spiral.

Rome

I wanted to plan a special treat for my mum and dad, to show them how much I appreciated their help and support, especially during these last few years. During my divorce from David, and everything I had gone through with Justin, they had provided me with so much emotional and practical support. They had listened to me pour out my heart and helped me so many times with moving my belongings and setting up a new home. I would have been lost without them.

My mum, being very controlling, would always assert her opinion about how the house should be decorated. I was nonetheless extremely grateful for her presence in these dark times. She has many great qualities and has always been there for me when I needed her.

I decided to bring my parents to Rome for three days, as my dad had always talked about wanting to go there. When I told them about my idea, they were over the moon. Even my mum, who hates travelling, was excited about the trip.

"Are you bringing anyone else?" she said. "You can't just go on holiday with us."

"Yes, I can," I said. "Anyway, I'm single. Who would I bring?"

"Bring a friend," she suggested. "That will make it more enjoyable for you."

"I am happy just going with you," I said.

My mum continued to insist that I bring a friend, so I invited Emma, a friend from Holywood. Since my mother and I have such a complicated relationship dynamic, it was a good idea to add Emma into the mix.

The four of us set off for Rome. It is truly a remarkable place. My dad was so excited when we arrived at the Vatican. The expression on his face was priceless. Our tour guide was brilliant and had the most exquisite Italian accent.

At the end of the Vatican tour, he said, "My dear, you look bravissimo, but how did you manage to walk around this tour all this time in those high-heeled boots?"

I laughed. "That's me," I said. "To me, these are comfortable."

Now it was his turn to laugh. "You are remarkable," he said.

"She never wears flats," my dad said. "We're just used to it."

My mum and I went shopping afterwards, so I continued walking around in those boots for many more hours. To this day, I love to wear high heels. They make me feel powerful and sexy.

We spent three great days in Rome, and my parents loved every moment. We all were particularly bowled over by the Colosseum, another magnificent piece of history. I have visited Rome three times since then, and each time I have been blown away by its architecture and history, and the simple, elegant style of the Italians. It truly is one of my favorite European cities.

On our last night, we went to a stunning Italian restaurant with awesome views over the city. Halfway through dinner, my mum started in on my dad over something stupid and she just wouldn't let up.

"Why are you doing this when we are having such a lovely time?" I asked her.

This landed on deaf ears. When my mum had mood swings, it was impossible for anyone else to level her out. My mum's behavior put a damper on our last night in Rome. I felt bad that Emma had to witness this, but I also found it validating. I felt that my mum would sometimes turn on us for no reason, and having Emma there helped confirm that I wasn't imagining it.

Looking back on it now, I understand that my mother must have felt very vulnerable being so far from home. She always was afraid to leave her comfort zone, and that is why she rarely traveled. Despite this glitch on the last evening, we all shared many beautiful moments in Rome, and I cherish my memories of this trip.

Nights in Marbella

That whole first year after Justin and I split up, I went to Marbella many times with the girls. I always spent way too much money. Apart from therapy, this was my only way of dealing with the pain. Sometimes we would stay in Marbella for a week, but mostly we would go there for a long weekend, flying out on Friday morning and returning on Monday evening. This was hard enough on the liver. During this time, Justin and I were in minimal contact. He knew how to get to me, and I knew getting too close would put me in danger of giving in. I felt it was best not to see him or speak to him.

Whenever the girls and I visited Marbella, it always was great fun. We would go to Puerto Banús for the weekend and stay in a lovely hotel. We would shop, eat, drink, and sunbathe. It was just what I needed at the time. When we went out, I would get lots of attention from men. Most of them were players, so I wasn't interested, but I still had fun winding them up.

One evening, a man was chatting me up when I noticed he was wearing a wedding ring.

"Are you married?" I asked him.

"Yeah," he said. "So what?"

"Then you can piss off," I said. "I feel sorry for your wife, you cheating git. I want nothing to do with you."

One of my friends told me to calm down.

"No," I said. "I bet his wife wouldn't be too happy if she knew what he was up to."

It made me very angry. I don't understand these people who get married and then just do whatever they want, whilst expecting their partners to remain faithful.

One weekend, we were staying at the Marbella Beach Club, a beautiful five-star resort a few miles outside the port. We would relax by the pool and talk about men and clothes and discuss our plans for the night. To an onlooker, we may have appeared to be ladies of leisure, but we all had great jobs and worked very hard.

On this night, we had decided to go to the Piano Bar, a popular nightspot with a great singer. It was usually filled with groups of men who had come to Puerto Banús to play golf, and groups of women who wanted to dance and have fun. The atmosphere was always electric. We walked along the waterfront, admiring the beautiful, suntanned people, exclusive designer shops, and luxury cars and yachts. It was always exciting to see how the other half lived.

A group of guys started shouting to us from the deck of an eighty-foot yacht. "Hi, girls! Come aboard for drinks!"

"Just ignore them," I told my friends. "Keep walking."

My friends were enjoying the attention.

"They look fit."

"Yeah, let's go and join them."

"No," I said, "Just leave it. Walk on."

We decided to first go to Sinatra's, which was also a very lively spot. About half an hour later, the guys from the yacht materialized in the bar and started chatting with us. They told us they were from Manchester. There were eight of them, and they were all quite attractive and full of fun, but I was suspicious of them.

"I bet they're all married," I said to one of my friends.

She replied, "Sure, so what if they are?"

"Yeah," I said, "just as long as they don't try anything on."

We had some fun with them.

A little while later, I said to the girls, "OK, let's go to the Piano Bar now."

We headed over there and enjoyed the rest of our night there.

The following evening, we ran into the lads from Manchester again. I found myself chatting to the one who owned the yacht, a handsome, tanned guy named Mark. He seemed like a lot of fun, and I found him attractive, but I couldn't get any real answers from him about his life. He kept saying he had a lot going on, and that he would be all over the news soon. Intrigued, I pressed for more details, but none of the guys would tell me what it was all about. We had a blast with them, and no one tried anything on with any of us. We all just had a laugh and danced the night away.

In the early hours of the morning, Mark offered us a lift to our hotel. He drove a white Bentley convertible with vanity plates that said CLAIMS. It seemed like an unusual word to put on your license plates. He dropped us off at our hotel, and we all watched him drive away.

"Oh my God!"

"Who the hell is this guy?"

"We need to find out."

On our last night, Mark said to me, "I just wanted to tell you I'm attracted to you. I am married, but if I wasn't, then things might be different. I hope you understand."

"Thank you," I said. "I'm flattered. I'm glad you are faithful to your wife. That's cool."

I liked that he was able to have fun with all of us girls without trying to get any of us into bed. In my experience, men in his position often play by their own set of rules.

About a week after we had returned home from Marbella, I was reading through the *Sunday Times*. I came upon a full-page spread about Mark Langford, a bankrupt businessman who was being investigated by HMRC for tax evasion, after his company had collapsed under £100M of debt.

The guy in the photos was Mark from Manchester. I could hardly believe my eyes. His company was called The Accident Group, and it dealt in compensation claims insurance—ambulance chasing, essentially. I remembered his vanity plates. The article mentioned that he had fired his 2,500 employees via text messaging.

I phoned up all the girls and said, "Go out and buy the Sunday Times right now! You will not believe it."

They were as shocked as I had been. We had all thought he was a nice man. Although I knew Marbella is full of people who are dodging something or hiding out, I couldn't believe we had actually met one of them.

Years later, I read in the papers that he had died in a car accident at the age of forty-two. It appeared that his life had been spiraling out of control in those last few years. I remembered him dancing and joking around with us all those nights in Marbella. I wondered if those were some of the last times when he was happy.

Back when I was apartment hunting in Marbella, my estate agent had introduced me to a polite and charming man. He was half-Italian, originally from London, and was now based in Marbella. He invited me out to dinner, and we hit it off as friends. He was an attentive listener and always gave good advice. He owned several luxury apartments and a magnificent villa. On many occasions, the girls and I stayed at one of his properties. He always refused payment. We called him Mr. T.

One evening, Mr. T took me to a beautiful restaurant by the sea and I told him all about what had happened with Justin.

He said, "You are in so much pain. You really need to get over this, as you will not be able to have a relationship otherwise."

Mr. T was a kind man, a great artist, and an animal lover. He was also seriously addicted to cocaine.

He once said, "Denise, you are high on life. I need cocaine to give me a high."

That made me feel sad for him. I had never touched drugs and feared getting involved with anything like that.

One evening, we all went to an amazing nightclub. It was an exclusive members' club, up in the mountains. The décor was sumptuous, and the music was out of this world. At the time, I was still in the throes of my post-divorce blues. My therapy sessions with Clare were helping a lot, but they were also bringing up a lot of painful emotions for me. I had been trying to numb my pain with shopping and alcohol, but they were not helping that much. I needed something to make me feel better.

So, when Mr. T handed me the sachet of white powder and said, "Just try it," I thought it might be just the thing to lift me out of my funk.

My friend and I skipped into the ladies' room like two children with a brand-new toy. I will never forget the high. I felt ready to take on the world. My friend and I danced until the sun came up, and then danced some more.

At eight in the morning, as we left the club, my friend said, "Where are we going now?"

"Bed," I said. "I don't know about you, but that's where I'm headed."

It was a beautiful night, but the comedown lasted for days. This was something I had to try for myself, but now I knew it wasn't for me. I felt it was something I didn't need in my life.

From Cyprus to Los Angeles

One night at the Piano Bar in Marbella, I met Jim, a tall, well-spoken Londoner with salt-and-pepper hair. He immediately struck me as very articulate and attractive. He had a distinguished air and a huge presence about him, but he was also very fun and down-to-earth. There was an instant spark between us. It had been over a year since the split with Justin, and Jim was the first man I thought I might be interested in. We had great fun together that evening, and he asked me to meet up again the following night. I gave him my number, and we soon embarked upon a relationship.

Over the next few months, we met up in Spain a couple of times. Some weekends he flew to Belfast to see me, and I visited him in London as well. He lived just off Kensington High Street, a main shopping street right in the heart of it all. A real London boy, he brought me to all the top restaurants and to Chinawhite, an exclusive VIP members-only club that I had wanted to visit for the longest time.

Jim was heavyset, but he carried it well and was always dressed to the nines. He was great fun and always looked very handsome, but I just wasn't all that in love with him. This was partly because I would often compare him to Justin, who I was still very hung up on. This was wrong of me, but I couldn't help it.

Jim was a lovely guy, and I really enjoyed spending time with him. I was fine with having a long-distance relationship, as I wasn't ready for anything too heavy. One day, Jim invited me to spend a week at a friend's villa in Cyprus with him and his crazy friend, Karl. I wasn't too sure about it, so I talked it over with my mum.

She said, "Go away with him and see how you feel. You have got to move on with your life. Just go."

I flew to London and spent the night at Jim's apartment, and the next day we flew to Cyprus. It was strange being at the airport with him, as I had spent the last five years travelling with Justin. This had always been very special and memorable, as planning trips was Justin's love language. Jim told me that Karl had invited two girls from Los Angeles to join us at the end of the week. This news caught me off-guard. I was excited to have other women to hang out with, but I was also worried that they would be absolutely stunning, and this would make me feel bad about myself. At that time, I was always so hard on myself.

During those first few days with Jim and his friends, I didn't feel any pressure to dress up. I was relaxing in my shorts and T-shirt, with my hair in a ponytail, after a day in the sun, when the door to the villa opened. In walked two gorgeous, glamorous, quintessentially LA women. They both had spray tans and long blond hair, cascading down their backs in perfect beach waves. High heels, tight jeans, and designer bags and luggage. They were larger than life. I instantly felt awful and insecure.

I thought, *Oh my God, how will I get through these next few days?*

The cuter one was called Barbie. She had large brown eyes and a fabulous figure. The other girl, Jenny, was also extremely pretty, but Barbie had the stronger personality. I could tell that she was the dominant one. They were both originally from Scotland, so they had lively personalities. I was instantly drawn to Barbie's confident nature, and we hit it off straight away.

The next day, we went out on Jim's friend's yacht, and I got to know both women a bit better. They sashayed onto the boat wearing bikinis, hats, heels, and full makeup. Their bodies glistened with suntan lotion. There I was, in my flat flipflops, shorts, no hat, and no makeup. I looked like a little nerd beside them. As they pranced around the boat, they were so sexy. I was in awe of them both. Even though I felt so unsexy and unglamorous compared to these two LA babes, I really enjoyed their company. I started to relax and stop worrying about my appearance.

Jim said, "You are getting on great with the girls."

"Yeah," I said, "they are great fun."

I got the feeling he wasn't really warming up to them. Barbie was very controlling and liked to get her own way. She was fairly demanding towards the guys. We had a lovely time together, but I had the sense that the girls weren't enjoying themselves all that much sometimes. Barbie had been dating Karl for a short time, but she seemed to have gone off him. I had probably gone off Jim also.

Barbie was very keen for me to visit LA. She told me she lived in a beachfront condo in Marina del Rey. By all accounts, it sounded like she had an amazing lifestyle. She worked for a millionaire who owned a fleet of private jets. She managed the jets, along with all the needs of the superstars who rented them. I was totally blown away by her. I thought that meeting her was exactly what I needed right then, to take my mind off Justin and help me envision a different life.

When I arrived back home, I ended my relationship with Jim. I just was not feeling it and I wanted to be free to enjoy my life. I was still trying to fix my heart and I didn't really trust men, so I felt I needed to be on my own. Barbie and I were on the phone most nights, chatting and having the craic. I found her very amusing, and I was intrigued by her.

A month later, I boarded a flight to LA. I was super excited, as I had never been there before, and I knew she would show me a great time. It felt very empowering to be jetting off by myself to spend two weeks in LA. And, thanks to my friend who worked for British Airways and got me a great deal, I was in business class. I was seated next to a lovely, interesting guy, and we spent the entirety of the flight chatting and drinking wine.

When I arrived at the airport, Barbie collected me in her Mercedes convertible, looking as glamorous as ever.

She said, "I hope you didn't drink on the flight. We're going out to dinner in one of the best restaurants in Beverly Hills."

I decided not to mention what I had been up to for the last nine hours.

When we arrived at her luxury condo overlooking the marina, she said, "Let's have some champagne before we go out!"

I could hardly keep my eyes open, but I just went along with it.

She whipped out a bottle of Cristal and said, "I just lifted this off my boss's plane."

I laughed. "Cool!"

Having never sampled Cristal before, I was a happy camper. We got changed and headed to Beverly Hills. I felt like a child in a candy store as we sailed down Rodeo Drive in all its fabulousness. The restaurant was fabulous. Halfway through dinner, I really started to fade. Jet lag washed over me. I felt like I was on another planet.

Barbie was like a female version of Justin. She was every bit as brash, forward, confident, controlling, and manipulative as he was.

I told myself, *That's OK. I just won't marry her. I can see who she is, but I enjoy her company. She makes me laugh and is showing me a new world.*

This was the start of our friendship. Barbie and I just gelled. We had an amazing connection. In the time to come, I would go to LA many times to visit her, and she would show me a part of life I would not have experienced otherwise. I had met her at exactly the right time. I had been through enough with the men in my life, and I was ready to live, travel, take risks, and see the world.

I felt shamed by Justin's affair and our subsequent divorce, and I was certain everyone was talking about me. I wanted to get away from it all. Perhaps running away was the only way I could deal with the pain. My employers were very understanding about my taking time off to travel. They knew what I was going through and had sympathy for me. It was a small company, in which everyone worked together closely, so they knew Justin well. It helped that I had a lot of ongoing sales coming in.

Whenever I wasn't traveling, I continued attending weekly sessions with my therapist, Clare.

Clare told me, "You are a highly intuitive person, so you must start listening to your gut. Never doubt your instincts."

I knew she was right. The night Justin had embarked upon his affair, I had known it in my heart. I could feel it. From that day forward, I started listening more carefully to my instincts. Yet I didn't always heed them.

I had started speaking with Justin again. I believed he was truly sorry for what he had done, and I knew he would be there for me if I ever needed anything. In a strange way, I have always looked up to him. Except for when it comes to matters of the heart, I have always felt that he has all the answers.

Justin was still trying to persuade me to take him back. He made promises, showered me with presents, and offered to take me on vacation, but I stayed strong. I didn't want to get hurt again, but it was hard to resist him. Many times, I asked myself if I should take him back. And, even if I should take him back, could I?

I had once told him, "Someday I will be happy. I'm just looking for someone who'll love me and be faithful to me, so I will find the person who's right for me. Your expectations are somewhat unrealistic, so you may never find that person."

Although I will never know whether he would have betrayed me again, I can certainly hazard a guess. Being cheated on doesn't exactly work wonders for one's self esteem, and mine had not been that high to begin with. And yet, I had enough strength to keep myself from getting back together with him. I knew I deserved to be with someone who would treat me well always, instead of only when it suited them.

What Happens in Vegas

By this time, I had settled into my new life. I loved my dogs and my house, and I felt secure and complete without a boyfriend. At this point in time, I associated romantic relationships with anxiety, stress, and pain, so I felt much happier being unattached. I would go on dates with various men, but I did not connect emotionally with any of them. Besides, I was still comparing everyone to Justin, so I knew I needed to spend more time healing myself.

I was working hard. I often vacationed in Marbella, and I flew out to see Barbie once or twice a year. Every time I went to see her, she had a new man in her life and a witty moniker for him. I greatly enjoyed our friendship. She's strong, funny, sexy, and doesn't give a shit about what anyone might think of her.

LA seemed to be a breeding ground for people's insecurities. It is populated by beautiful people, yet so many of them constantly undergo plastic surgery and other cosmetic procedures, to try to appear younger or to appropriate a perceived ideal.

One afternoon during my visit, Barbie said, "Want to go to Vegas? We can just get a domestic flight."

"Yeah, why not?" I said. "I have never been there."

I was excited to visit Las Vegas and find out what it was all about. Our flight on Southwest Airlines was like a party bus. The flight attendants were dressed in shorts. They sang: "What happens in Vegas stays in Vegas. Look out for that Vegas Burn!"

I laughed, thinking, *What on earth are they on about? This is going to be some place.*

As we disembarked, I felt as if I had walked into an oven. No one ever warns you that Vegas is right in the middle of a desert. It was July, and the heat was sweltering. My jeans were instantly plastered to my skin, and I could feel sweat running down my legs. I felt like a chicken that was starting to roast.

The atmosphere in Vegas is so exciting. The city truly never sleeps. We had a lot of fun and met so many gorgeous men. One night, I met a hot doctor from Chicago who bought me Long Island iced teas until I was about to fall over. Barbie had already headed off with some Romeo. I thanked Dr. Windy City, went back to the hotel room, and hit the hay.

In the morning I was woken by a ringing phone. I could hardly lift my head off the pillow.

It was Barbie. "I'm at Caesar's Palace."

We were staying at the Bellagio.

"Can you come over with my jeans and a sweater?" she asked. "I just can't do the walk of shame in this dress."

"Yeah," I said. "But give me an hour. I am dying here."

"Sure, no problem," she said.

An hour later, she phoned again. "Oh my God, where are you?"

"OK, OK. I won't be long."

My head was crashing and thudding like a pinball machine as I walked through the hotel lobby. I hopped into a cab and asked the driver to take me to Caesar's Palace, which turned out to be directly next door to the Bellagio. I was so embarrassed.

I phoned Barbie. "I'm here," I said.

"I'm in the penthouse," she said. "Come up."

I got in the elevator and rode it to the top. I knocked on the door. After a few minutes, it opened to reveal a grand reception room, with a banquet table that could have seated twenty-four people. Behind it was a sweeping panoramic view of the Vegas skyline. I was blown away. I handed Barbie her clothes and she disappeared into one of the rooms to get changed. I sat there, making polite conversation with the guy she had hooked up with. In his dark glasses and white bathrobe, he looked like Andy Garcia.

Barbie emerged in her jeans and sweater. She winked at me and said, "Let's take off."

As soon as the elevator doors slid shut, she burst out laughing. She launched into a detailed and funny description of the sex they'd had the night before, as well as that morning. She asked me how things had gone with the doctor.

"Ah yeah, we had a lovely night, drinking Long Island iced tea and talking our heads off. It was good fun."

She must have thought I was a little square, but I had nothing to prove. I was protecting my heart, so I was happy to have had a fun conversation with the doctor. That was all I had wanted.

When it was time to catch our return flight, we were both totally exhausted. This was it—the Vegas Burn. It is rumored that the casinos pump oxygen into the air so you can stay up all night gambling, and that this is what causes the Vegas Burn, but it is a myth. Its origins can be traced to a Mario Puzo novel in which a fictitious hotel casino employs this trick. It doesn't make sense and would be illegal, as pumping pure oxygen into an enclosed space makes everything inside it more flammable and increases the risk of fire. As casinos allow guests to smoke inside, there is absolutely no way they would do this.

However, they do scent the air and keep the air-conditioning cranked all the way up, to keep gamblers alert and awake. Inside the casinos are no clocks and no windows, so your sense of time and your circadian rhythms get discombobulated. When you leave, it hits you with a bang. Our flight to LA was delayed for hours, and there were no vacant seats in the waiting area by our departure gate. We lay on the floor in our gorgeous clothes like two rag dolls.

I believe people come into your life for a reason. After everything I had been through with Justin, Barbie came along and showed me another world, which was amazing. Building new friendships, exploring new places, and having innocent flirtations were all positive and empowering experiences that helped me to rebuild my confidence.

The Captain

I was meeting some very nice men, but I didn't want to get involved with any of them. I kept faithfully attending my weekly therapy sessions with Clare, as I felt she helped keep me on track. Much of our work together involved learning to practice self-love and self-care. For me, these were the hardest concepts to grasp.

I had always felt that love was centered on other people—I was supposed to love them and try to earn their affection and approval. I never knew that love should begin with me. Clare helped me to realize no one else can love you until you truly love yourself. But at this stage in my life, I didn't yet know how to put this into practice.

My friend Lisa (who I had met through Justin) was also recently divorced. She's fun and she loves food, wine, and skiing, so we started vacationing together. We spent ten days skiing at St Anton am Arlberg, in the Tyrolean Alps, and both came back fifteen pounds heavier from all the food and drink. The food in Austria is fabulous, and no matter how much you ski, it's not enough to burn off all the calories you consume.

One day, Lisa asked me, "Do you feel like going somewhere a bit different?"

I said, "Yeah, let's see what we can get up to."

I went to see the travel agent, and she told me about a cruise to Bermuda. I had never been on a cruise before, and it sounded like a lot of fun. The cruise would depart from Philadelphia, spend two days at sea, two in Bermuda, and another two sailing back to Philly. Lisa loved the idea, and we decided to go for it.

We headed off to Philly and spent one night there. The following morning, we boarded the cruise ship. After freshening up in our cabin, we went straight to the pool to sunbathe and have cocktails. The ship was full of starry-eyed couples, who were being touchy-feely, but I tried not to let this bother me. I was on a cruise ship for the first time, and there wasn't a cloud in the sky.

Lisa is athletic looking, with cropped hair and a very fit body. She usually dresses in casual wear. I would come out to the pool in my glam bikini or a slinky dress, and she would laugh and say, "We are an odd couple."

Our personal styles couldn't have been more different, but we were similar in temperament and always got on very well.

On our second night at sea, we joined some other people for dinner. They were all quite boring. I remember thinking, *Where's the craic?* I asked them whether they knew of any good clubs in Bermuda, and they told us about a great little club.

I winked at Lisa and said, "That's where we'll be going when we get to Bermuda."

Later that night, we ventured down to the ship's nightclub. It was pretty crap, but at least they had music. We had become fond of lychee martinis, so we ordered some and sipped them at the bar. An officer came over to us and said, "The captain would like to buy you girls a drink."

"Ooh," we said. "Thank you."

Another round of lychee martinis arrived. Before long, the ship's captain appeared in his white uniform. He was tall and tanned. "Hi, girls! My name is Dimitris. What are you two doing on this ship? Are you lesbians?"

Lisa and I laughed. "We are just good friends," I said.

"We don't often see two single ladies on this ship," he said.

"Yeah," I said. "I can see that it is mostly couples."

We chatted with Dimitris and had a few drinks with him. Then we headed back to our cabin to get some sleep.

In the morning, we awoke to the sound of a phone ringing. I jumped up and said, "What's that, Lisa?"

She said, "It's a phone. But like, a real one."

We searched the cabin until we found the phone. When I answered it, I heard a deep voice saying, "Baby, this is your captain speaking. Come to the pool bar." The caller hung up.

I said, "Oh my God, that was him! What do we do?"

"Come on," she said, "let's go and see what he wants!"

When we arrived at the pool, we were greeted by hot, blaring sunshine. We realized the ship had already docked in Bermuda.

Dimitris was standing there, looking very handsome in his dazzling white suit and cap. He put his arm around me and said, "Hey, baby! Can I get you girls a nice glass of wine?"

Everyone at the bar was looking at us.

"Ah, OK," I said, "why not?"

"Sure, we are on our holidays," Lisa said.

Dimitris said, "I will take you girls to the beach. I know a beautiful beach with pink sand."

I was already so excited about seeing Bermuda. Having a handsome guy volunteering to show us around made it ten times more exciting.

Lisa said, "Denise, this has made our holiday so much better!"

"I couldn't agree more," I replied.

The three of us set off to the beach. We spent a beautiful day in the sun together. After that, we were inseparable. Dimitris made sure that our time in Bermuda was unforgettable. Bermuda is breathtaking, and so regal. Traces of its English heritage are reflected everywhere—even on the Bermuda shorts the men wear. Dimitris and I had a wonderful holiday romance. We kept things light and fun, nothing too intense.

When our cruise ship departed Bermuda, he brought us onto the bridge. It was amazing to observe. Steering a ship out of port requires such concentration that no one on board is allowed to speak. As the ship started gliding away, I looked out over the sea and thought, *Wow, I am a lucky girl to be experiencing all of this. Bad things happen sometimes, but then good things come along to help take away the pain.*

Life was good, and I was having the time of my life being footloose and fancy-free. I really enjoyed my time on the ship with Lisa and the captain. On our last day on the ship, the captain said, "Ladies, you are both coming back in two weeks for a free cruise."

Lisa and I looked wide-eyed at each other for a moment.

"Yes, yes!"

"We would love that!"

We skipped off the ship like two delighted schoolgirls.

I returned home and went back to work. Dimitris would phone me at all hours of the day and night, from the ship's satellite phone in the middle of the ocean. I was flattered by his interest in me, and his constant attention made me feel good. Two weeks later, Lisa and I headed back to Philadelphia and boarded the cruise ship. He had put us in the top cabin, complete with its own Jacuzzi and a fully stocked bar.

Dimitris said, "You Irish need your drink."

I wouldn't argue with that.

Lisa said, "Denise, I could pinch myself."

I said, "I know! This is so brilliant."

Throughout the cruise, Dimitris spoiled us both rotten. We basked in every moment of it.

One day, he said, "I am taking one of the ship's lifeboats to go fishing with two of the officers. You girls can come and sunbathe. I will bring lunch from the kitchen, and champagne."

Lisa and I had a ball. We loved sailing around the beautiful little islands. Dimitris and the officers caught some fish, and the next day they had the kitchen serve it to us for lunch. What a fantastic experience it was! It was like a dream.

After that, Dimitris came to Ireland to visit me, and I went to Athens to see him and meet his family. He invited me onto the ship for a cruise around the Caribbean, so I flew to Miami to meet him. It was very exciting to be known as the girlfriend of the captain, as you received special treatment from everyone. Dimitris treated me to spa facials and showered me with gifts. He gave me so many beautiful things. In Miami, he bought me a pink Louis Vuitton scarf, as he knew that I love pink.

Over time, I discovered that Dimitris had two sides. He was loving and caring, and he was also extremely jealous and possessive. It soon became clear that his gift-giving had two sides as well. Although he gave gifts out of generosity, he was also trying to own me. Whenever he could not get me on the phone, he went mad. If he was annoyed about something, the silent treatment would go on for days.

By now, I had learned to recognize this type of emotionally abusive behavior as a red flag. I discussed all of this with Clare in my weekly therapy sessions. I realized that yet again, I had fallen for the same type of man for whom I always fell—a person who wanted to control me.

I was aware that I had slipped back into the type of relationship dynamic I was trying so hard to avoid. On the other hand, I really liked him, so I continued dating him, even as I saw myself falling into the same patterns I had learned from my relationship with my mother and which I had carried over to all my key relationships. I became distraught whenever he was angry with me. Even though I understood that he was angry because he couldn't control me, and not because I had done anything wrong, I would phone him and apologize.

One night, I was out at a club in Belfast when he rang my cellphone and said, "Get home now."

"No, I won't," I said. "I am out having fun and you are in the middle of the ocean on a ship, so piss off."

The following day I woke up to a string of email messages, in which he demanded that I phone him. Something inside me suddenly woke up, and I decided not to call. He was trying to control me from another part of the world, and for months I had allowed it to continue. What had started out as a fun romance was rapidly devolving into a dysfunctional relationship. While I was grateful for everything we had shared, I knew it was time to walk away.

I decided to make a conscious effort to put down some roots. I got settled in my house in Holywood and stopped running off to far-flung places at the drop of a hat. At this stage, my work life was every bit as demanding as it ever had been, as I was managing a roster of important clients, including many blue-chip companies. I had started to make more friends in my area. I joined the gym at a nearby hotel. All that traveling had been just what I needed after the dissolution of my marriage. It had helped me to broaden my horizons and allowed me some space in which to heal and grow. And now, I needed to create a life at home.

On A Wing and A Prayer

I wanted to start my own business brokering print and design. As I worked for a small printing firm with limited manufacturing capacity and ever-increasing sales, we outsourced a lot of our print. In all practicality, although I worked in sales, I was both purchasing and selling print. Before long, I realized I could work for myself instead. I talked this over with Justin, as we were on friendly terms by this time. I have always valued his business acumen, and he gives good advice.

Justin encouraged me to go for it. "I know you can do it," he said. "And if you need any help, I am here for you."

I liked having a friendship with Justin. As a friend he is honest and loyal, and he makes me feel safe. At this stage, I told myself I was keeping him in my life because I needed him as a sounding board and consultant on various matters, but there was more to it. In the back of my mind, the possibility always lingered. Perhaps one day I would forgive him and take him back. I just wasn't there yet.

I decided I would name my company Robinson Consulting, and I had some business cards made up. This was about the extent of my planning. I discussed my intentions with only one customer, who also happens to be my friend. She said she would keep giving me all her business, and this gave me a final push to go ahead with it. As I had earned a corporate salary my whole working life up to that point, it was scary to leave that behind and try to make it on my own without a safety net. But I had to do what was right for me, and I knew this was what I wanted to do.

I notified my employer of my decision. I told them I would take over the lease on the Mercedes instead of leaving it with them until the end of the contract. I offered to keep giving them business, but they declined. I guess it wouldn't have made sense for them to do so, as it would have narrowed their profit margin.

I set up my business as a consulting firm, through which I subcontracted the design element to a freelance graphic designer and outsourced the print work to various printers. When I look back on it now, I can see that it must have taken some balls to strike out on my own. I was paying off a mortgage by myself and had exited the company without any real confirmation that my customers would keep working with me. But at the time, I took it all in stride.

I contacted all my customers, some of whom were at large blue-chip companies, and every single one of them said, "Of course we'd love to keep working with you. We know *you*. We have a relationship with you."

That's how I learned that people buy from people and not from companies. I was delighted that they trusted me to manage their print. When my first purchase order appeared in my inbox, I was over the moon. It was for £12K and had been placed by Transport NI. I almost wept with joy. This was incredibly affirming and fueled my determination and drive to make my business succeed.

Before long, printers were contacting me for work. I was glad I had pushed myself to make this move. In my first year I turned over £450K, working from my kitchen table. I hired a part-time bookkeeper to create invoices, pay the VAT, and pay suppliers. Whenever necessary, I would chase payments. As most companies paid within thirty days, there was rarely an issue. I was flying high and never looked back.

One evening, Barbie phoned to tell me she was getting married to the plastic surgeon she had been dating for some time now.

"Congratulations!" I exclaimed. "Ah Barbie, that's beautiful news. I'm so happy and delighted for you."

"You have to come to LA for the wedding," she said. "I won't take no for an answer."

I told her I could not afford to take any time off at that moment, as I was at a crucial stage of growing my business. Things had really taken off, and I was pretty much the whole company, so I had to be there to run things. I explained the situation and hoped she would understand. Just then, her controlling personality emerged full force, and she launched into an enormous guilt trip, citing all the things she had done for me.

Finally, I said, "OK. I will see what I can do."

I had given in because I wanted to be a good friend, and because I was still predisposed to submit to people who have control issues. I worked things out so I could be absent from my business for four days, and I managed to acquire a British Airways economy ticket for £300. Los Angeles is a long way to go for just four days, but that was how it would have to be. At least I had saved some money on the flight.

At the airport check-in counter, I said, "May I please have a window seat? I am a little claustrophobic."

The ground steward said, "There are hardly any seats remaining. You should have checked in online."

This was the beginning of online check-ins. "I'm sorry," I said, "I didn't realize."

"All I have is an aisle seat and a center seat."

"Oh no—I will find that very hard to take for ten hours."

"Hold on a moment," he said, clicking away on the keyboard. "Lady, it's your lucky day. You're keeping me in a job by checking in here, so I have upgraded you to Business Class."

"What? No way!" I wanted to jump over the counter and kiss him.

He handed me my boarding card. "Enjoy!"

The wedding was magnificent. The couple exchanged vows at a cliff's edge overlooking Laguna Beach, and hosted a lavish reception at the Ritz-Carlton, Laguna Niguel. Barbie was radiant, beaming with happiness. She looked perfect, like a doll. I could tell that she was extremely in love with her husband, and I was delighted for them both.

As lovely as it was to see her and to be back in LA, by the end of my stay I was keen to get back home to my business. When I arrived back at home, I was slightly jetlagged but ready to rock.

By this time, I had been in therapy for about two years. I felt I had learned a lot from Clare and was in a much better place these days. I decided it was time to stop seeing her and work on myself independently. My business was flourishing, my friendships were amazing, and I was feeling happy and settled in my new life.

I still had a lot of underlying issues around believing in myself as an individual. At this stage I was earning more money than I ever had. I was spending a fair amount on clothes and luxury items, as I felt I had to dress and present myself in a certain fashion to be considered attractive. Looking back at myself, I can see how insecure I was then. I did not yet know how to love myself, and I never could see myself as others did. I was smart, beautiful, and successful, but I did not value these qualities in myself. Without the material trappings, I felt I was not good enough. I still couldn't love myself just for being me.

When you have spent most of your life doubting yourself and struggling with feelings of inferiority, it is hard to turn that around. My inferiority complex was rooted in the psychological damage my mother had inflicted, during my childhood and into my early adulthood. She had put me down in front of my friends and partners, and this had made me feel I was never good enough. Clare had helped me to identify the unhealthy patterns, dynamics and attitudes that were holding me back, but I would still need to do a lot of work and travel farther along my journey before I could start loving me.

The Next Big Love

At thirty-eight, I owned my home and was running a successful business. Life was good. It had been four years since I had split up with Justin, but I still wasn't looking for The One. I was just dating and enjoying the single life. I loved working for myself, traveling, and having fun with my friends. I had made some new friends in my area and some through work, so I always had a full social calendar. My parents were always around, and they visited me most weekends.

My friend Kathy phoned me on a Saturday afternoon. "Do you fancy going into the village for lunch and some drinks?"

"Yeah, why not?" I said, unaware that this would mark the beginning of the next six years of my life, after which my heart would truly be destroyed.

Over an extended liquid lunch in a cozy little bar, Kathy told me she had been seeing a new guy. He was out with a friend and would be coming to meet us later. We spent the afternoon shooting the breeze and drinking. It was early evening when her guy showed up. He had brought his friend along. As they walked in, I looked at the friend and thought, *Wow*. I felt an almost magnetic attraction, and I could sense that he felt it too.

The friend was called Steve. He had blond hair and that posh schoolboy look and was extremely well spoken. He said he lived in Holywood, but I had never seen him before. I felt very relaxed, but I could tell he was holding back. Although there was a lot of chemistry between us, neither of us acted on it.

We all had a few drinks before heading over to the Indian restaurant next door. It was all very civilized, and we didn't stay out late that night. I went home thinking, *Gosh, now that was a handsome man.*

The next day was Sunday. Kathy phoned and suggested going for a walk with the dogs. She lived just down the beach from me.

"How about that Steve?" Kathy said, with a twinkle in her eye. "He's good-looking, isn't he?"

I said, "Yeah, lovely. How have we never met him before?"

"Yeah," she said. "You know, until recently, he was married. He has kids and everything. I guess that's why he wasn't out and about much."

I had sensed that he wasn't looking to date anyone, and now I could understand why. As we walked our dogs on the beach, laughing and dissecting the events of the previous night, who should come running towards us at top speed but the man himself.

"Oh my God, look who it is!" I hissed at Kathy.

She broke off mid-sentence. "This is embarrassing."

Steve ran up to us and jogged in place as he said what a great night it had been. I grinned and nodded, trying not to stare at his chest, which was conveniently outlined by his sweat-soaked T-shirt.

"What a fit man," we both sighed as he ran off. "What a coincidence."

We giggled like two teenagers.

A few weeks passed. One Friday evening after work, I went to the local pub with a group of friends. It's a real old man's pub where many people from the village congregate after work on a Friday evening. As I ordered my gin and tonic, I glanced across the bar and there was Steve. *This is so crazy,* I thought. *I have lived in the village for four years and had never seen him before, and now he is everywhere.*

He came straight over and was all chat. I could feel the connection between us sparking and buzzing like electricity. He seemed different from anyone I had ever dated before. There was something special about him. I introduced him to the friends I was with, and a few of them thought he was incredibly posh. He was quite posh, but he wasn't pretentious. He was classy and educated, yet gentle and understated.

I learned that he owned a well-established family business, one that I had heard of over the years. The craic was great, and there was the usual carry-on after the pub, as there was no other place to go, and we didn't want the night to end.

Kathy said, "Let's all go back to my house for a party."

Steve said, "Can I come along?"

"Yes, of course you can," I said.

A group of around ten people went back to Kathy's for drinks, music, and dancing. I could tell Steve was quite tipsy. He was getting more flirtatious with me.

He said, "I find you very attractive and very sexy."

I laughed it off, the way I always did when men described me as sexy. I didn't see myself this way, and I could not take a compliment. "Well, it's pretty late," I said. "I need to go home to my dogs. I hate leaving them home alone for too long."

He grabbed me and kissed me deeply. He was a great kisser—passionate without being sloppy—and his lips were surprisingly soft and plump. I wanted that kiss to go on forever. It felt so good I could have eaten him right up, but I handed him my business card and headed off. In the taxi home, I asked myself, *Could this man be the one for me?*

The next day was Saturday. I was having breakfast and relaxing with the dogs, and the sun was shining through the window. I loved my house. It was an old Victorian house that still retained its cornicing and other antique features. I said to the dogs, "What shall we do today, guys?"

Of course, all they wanted was to be walked along the beach. I decided we would relax for a bit and then head to the beach, which was at the bottom of my road.

I lived in a beautiful part of Northern Ireland. People refer to it as the Gold Coast, as it is extremely picturesque and features many gorgeous homes. I love this area more than anywhere else I have lived, as I have a huge affinity with the sea. Especially after the breakup, I found it a very therapeutic place to spend my time.

As I was getting myself together to start the day, I received a text from an unknown number. "Would you like to have a cup of tea and tell me more about being a print consultant?"

This is the job title written on my business card, so I knew it had to be Steve. And who else would invite you out for a cup of tea?

I texted back: "Hi there! How are you feeling today?"

"Not too bad. Do you fancy meeting down at the gym?"

"Sure."

He phoned me to work out the details. It turned out that we were members of the same gym and spa, situated in a beautiful five-star hotel almost next door to my house. Coincidentally, this hotel is where David and I had held our wedding reception all those years ago.

I said I would need to walk the dogs first.

"No problem," he said, and we agreed on a time to meet.

As soon as I ended the call, I suddenly remembered that I was terribly hungover. I went and looked at myself in the bathroom mirror. *Oh my God, I thought, would you look at the state of me?*

Mascara was streaked halfway down my face, and my hair was sticking up as if I had been pulled through a haystack. I headed off to the beach with the doggies for a long, brisk walk. Then I rushed home, had a shower, and spruced up my appearance. The aim was to look stunning, of course, but also casual and relaxed. I didn't want to come across as some kind of dolly bird who would get all done up on a weekend afternoon.

Our date felt like a first date, butterflies and all. I had an inkling this would be the first of many dates. I could already tell I was more attracted to him than I ever had been to anyone else. Even the pure, animal attraction I'd felt for MJ was nothing compared to what I was feeling in that moment. Steve had the class and the looks, and I just loved his quiet, polite manner. Compared with Justin, Steve was much more reserved, and he didn't appear to have any domineering personality traits. He didn't give much away, but when he did, you felt it was genuine. I thought, *Perhaps this is just what I need.* I sensed that this was to be the start of my next big love. Little did I know he would be the biggest love of my life.

When we first started dating, it was early days for him. He was fresh out of his marriage, and he felt guilty for having left his wife, even though he had known for a long time that he was unhappy. He always spoke very highly of his wife, and she sounded like a genuinely lovely lady.

I was happy with taking things slow. I didn't want to deal with too much of his emotional baggage, as I was still recovering from the breakdown of my own marriage. Before long, he began to move things forward at a quicker pace and our relationship grew more intense. Soon he was texting me at all hours of the day. I should have recognized this pattern, and perhaps I did, but I could not resist him.

We had this crazy chemistry. It was unlike anything I had ever felt before. I will never forget the first time we had sex. It was the best feeling of my life. I could not stop smiling. I loved the way he made me feel. From that moment we could not keep our hands off each other.

Back then, we never went out together in public. He was a well-known businessman, and we lived in a small village. I didn't want anyone to think I had broken up his marriage, as this was not the case. We spent a lot of time at my place, chatting, drinking wine, and having the most amazing sex. I was so happy all the time. I was always smiling like a Cheshire cat. Nothing could get to me.

When we both were out in the local bar, we would try to stick with our respective friend groups and act normal, but he couldn't stay away. He would keep coming over to me, the attraction between us shining like a laser beam. It was magic. I felt I was being rewarded after all the heartache I had endured.

When he felt that enough time had passed that it would be acceptable for him to publicly get on with his life, he asked me to accompany him to the Down Royal Races. I loved the races, and I was ready for our relationship to be out in the open. I was getting sick of sneaking around.

Little did I know, it wasn't going to be that simple. Steve comes from old money, and many members of his extended family resided in our area. I knew about his family's business, but I hadn't known exactly the type of family he comes from. His ex-wife also comes from a lovely, well-known family. It was a massive thing that they had split up. Looking back on it now, I suppose everyone must have thought they would eventually get back together, and then he met me. We had great fun at the races, but tongues were wagging. Everyone knew that Steve had started dating some blonde, who was five years younger than he was.

The next morning, I was doing some last-minute packing for a girls' trip to Marbella when Steve phoned. He said his family was angry with him for getting involved with someone else so soon. He was very upset.

I thought, *I don't need this hassle*. Even though I felt that our relationship was the best thing that had ever happened to me, I wasn't prepared to deal with an onslaught of external pressure.

"If I'm being honest, I'm not sure I want to get involved in all of this," I said. "I am just about to head off to Marbella with Kathy and Jane. Let's talk about this when I am back."

"Please don't overreact," he said. "My family will come around. Everything will be fine, I promise."

After we ended the call, I realized I wasn't that worried about whether his family would ever change their views on our relationship. While it would be much harder for us if they stood in our way, this wasn't the primary issue. His apparent lack of autonomy over his own life was much more problematic. It was troubling to learn how much weight their opinions carried. Even if they eventually changed their minds and gave us their blessing, how would his family dynamic impact our relationship over time? Would they attempt to control other aspects of our lives?

If I hadn't been madly in love with him, I might have broken things off at this point. I was sick of being controlled by the people I dated, so I certainly didn't want to be controlled by someone's family. But I wasn't ready to give up on us. I would need some time to think things over, so I was glad to be heading off with my friends on vacation.

Options

As we checked into the Marbella Beach Club for the weekend, I thought, *This is exactly what I need right now*. Steve was constantly texting and phoning me. I asked him to give me some space and stopped taking his calls.

On our first day by the pool, a group of guys from London came over to where we were sunbathing and initiated conversation. They said they had come to Marbella to play tennis. I didn't engage with them. I just reclined on my chaise longue catching some rays while my friends chatted with them. After a while, I got into the pool.

One of the guys swam over to me and introduced himself as Lyndsay. He was Irish, from Cork, and lived in London, where he worked as a lawyer. He seemed smart and funny, and I was struck by his huge brown eyes. You could tell he played tennis, as he was tanned and muscular. We chatted for a while before climbing out of the pool and rejoining our friends. The craic was great. We all had quite a few cocktails. The guys asked us if we would meet up with them later, and we said we would.

That evening when we walked into the Piano Bar, they were already there, waiting for us. Lyndsay ran over to me and pulled me onto the dance floor. He was a terrific dancer, and we danced for hours. It was intoxicating, and I was very attracted to him, but I knew my heart belonged to Steve. At one point in the evening, Lyndsey tried to kiss me. I told him I was in a relationship. He took it well, and said we could just have fun and enjoy the night. We all drank a lot and had a ball.

The next day, when the guys had finished playing tennis, they came to the pool to find us. We sunbathed, drank, and chatted some more. Steve was still incessantly phoning and texting me. I told him I needed some time to think things over, which was true. Still, I felt a bit guilty. I really liked Lyndsay. Plus, as a single guy without any discernable baggage, he was looking pretty good to me. Steve, on the other hand, had an ex to whom he was still legally married, three children, a controlling mother, and his whole family already hated me. They were blaming me for the dissolution of his marriage, even though it had nothing to do with me.

On the last evening, I kissed Lyndsay. My friends told me I should carefully consider my options, as Lyndsay seemed great. If I decided not to pursue a relationship with him, I should be sure that Steve was right for me. My thoughts and emotions were in a muddle, and I didn't know what to do. Anyway, I was heading home, and he was heading back to London, so I would have time to think about it all.

When I arrived home, I was receiving texts from them both. I met up with Steve and was honest with him.

I said, "On holiday, I met someone I could have feelings for. He has no baggage. I'm really worried about whether I can take on all your baggage. I have been through so much with Justin. I just want an easy life."

He said, "Please don't think that way. I will never get back together with my ex-wife. In time, my family will come to accept it."

I said, "OK. Let me think about it."

I felt I needed to see Lyndsay under normal circumstances, away from the holiday feeling, to see whether there was something real between us. He offered to fly in on a Sunday, so we could spend the day together.

I picked up him at the airport and we had lunch and went for a walk. He was just as gorgeous and sweet as I remembered. I felt so confused. I didn't know what to do.

I was honest with him. I said, "I really like you and could see myself falling in love with you very easily. But I really love Steve, and he is right here. Long-distance relationships are hard."

Lyndsey said, "That's true. But look at everything you'll be taking on if you stay with him. That won't be easy, either."

"I know," I said. "I need to think about it."

I loved my time with Lyndsey, but when I dropped him off at the airport, I knew it was goodbye. Steve was the one for me. Even if it was going to be hard, I was willing to fight for our relationship, no matter what lay ahead.

I immediately went and told Steve I had chosen him. He was elated. From that moment on, we spent almost every night together. When he traveled to the UK for business, I often accompanied him. I'd fly over for the night and return the following day. We went on so many amazing holidays together, and I even brought him to LA to meet Barbie and her husband. We stayed with them in their Beverley Hills mansion. On that trip, we also went up to San Francisco.

Steve and I were like two peas in a pod. No matter what we were doing—vacationing in some tropical location, walking the dogs on the beach, or having a simple barbecue—it always felt perfect. We just loved being together.

One evening, I said to Steve, "Isn't it great that we can sit on this beach and do absolutely nothing, and just be happy and have amazing sex, and it's free?"

When you are so in love, nothing else matters. Every time I looked at Steve, I wanted to kiss him, touch him or jump on him. I was attracted to him twenty-four hours of the day. It was a level of attraction I had never experienced before. To me, he was simply gorgeous. I thought, *This is it. I know we will be together forever.*

Holding Pattern

When Steve and I had been dating for a year, I met his daughter and his two sons. They were beautiful kids. The boys were keen on sports and especially loved to play rugby. Mostly Steve attended their games by himself, and sometimes I joined him. Over time I formed great relationships with both his sons, but it proved difficult to form a bond with his daughter. I think she may have thought I was the reason her parents had split up. I guess she needed someone to blame.

When Steve and I had been together for three years, we decided there was no point in having two houses, especially as we always stayed together. We started talking about whether we should live together in his place. I was a little nervous about renting out my house, as I loved it and feared that a tenant might not care for it properly. Eventually, I agreed to move in with Steve and rent the house out for one year, just to see how it went.

As soon as I moved in with him, his mother and his daughter began making our lives much more difficult. His family never stopped regarding me as a homewrecker, even though I hadn't known Steve at the time his marriage had ended. Occasionally, I was invited to attend their family dinners, but I was never made to feel welcome. I didn't tick any of their boxes, in terms of the type of woman they would envision for him. I didn't come from old money, and I had not attended private school. Their biggest issue would have been that I am Catholic. They also strongly disapproved of my having been married twice before.

They made feel like a bad person. The more they picked me apart, the more I could feel all the old wounds reopening. I felt like I was disintegrating. I told Steve that I felt he was not standing up for me, and we argued about this a lot.

I would tell Steve, "Your family is never going to accept me."

He would always reply, "They will be fine in time, you'll see. I just think your moving into what used to be our family home has set them on overdrive."

I didn't understand how this observation was supposed to make me feel better, as it was too late now. Besides, moving in together had been primarily his idea. But it was true that there was too much history in Steve's house, so we decided to renovate it and put it up on the market. In hindsight, I should never have moved in, and we should have just gotten a new place together.

I set about renovating the house. I spent six months employing designers, builders, and painters to gut the place and start over from scratch, all while continuing to run my business. Here I came up against even stronger opposition, as the family hated the idea that I was changing the property to make it appear more modern, and the kids wanted it to stay the same. I can understand how the kids felt, as it was their childhood home, but the other people should have kept their noses out.

We completely transformed the house and put it up for sale. In the end, Steve's boys loved what I had done with it. I think his daughter also liked it, but she would never say too much. I tried so hard to gain her trust and build a relationship with her, but she simply did not like me. The more I tried, the more hostile she became towards me. I could not win, and it made me really start to doubt myself. My bubbly personality started to dwindle, as I felt I was never good enough. I did my best to become someone that I wasn't, just so I could fit into their lifestyle. When I spoke, I often wondered whether I was saying the right thing.

Things were up and down for a while. His family continued to interfere with our relationship, and we continued to argue about this. By now, Steve and I had been together for four years, and many of my friends who had been dating for a shorter time than we had were getting engaged.

When my friend Alison got engaged to the golfer Darren Clarke, I told Steve, "They have been together only a year and they are engaged."

He said, "We don't have to compare our relationship to anyone else's. Everyone moves at a different pace. We love each other. We don't need to rush into anything."

I began to worry that he did not see a future with me. I was forty-four, and I didn't want to spend time being in a relationship that wasn't going anywhere. Everyone I had dated had wanted to marry me, even before I was ready. For the first time, I was ready to get married, and now the other person didn't want to marry me.

Was his family getting inside his head? Or was there something wrong with me? Did he simply not feel that strongly about me? I started slipping back into my old, destructive patterns of thinking that if someone didn't return my love in the way I wanted, it meant that there was something wrong with me. I often felt insecure, and I became more needy. I started to lose myself a bit.

Steve had his routine nailed down. Every Saturday he played golf or went to watch his sons play rugby. He was also devoted to running and to working out at the gym. As I did my best to fit in around his schedule, I forgot about myself and what I needed.

I was also spending a lot of money on travelling with Steve, maintaining a certain lifestyle, and contributing to our living expenses. I felt pressured to keep up, as I never wanted him or his family to look down on me. I also wanted to make it clear that I was not relying on him in any way. I was never interested in his wealth. I loved him for who he was.

Shortly before Steve's mum passed away, she decreed that I was not to sit beside him at her funeral. She was his mother, and I was truly sad for his loss. I did my best to support him through his bereavement, though I didn't plan to attend the funeral, as I had been very hurt when I heard about her dying wish.

I spoke with my dad about all of this. My dad had never really warmed to Steve, as he felt Steve was a conformist, who had stepped out of his comfort zone to be with me but wasn't willing to stand up for me for fear of displeasing his family. My dad knew how Steve's mum had disrespected me.

He said, "You must rise above it. Go to the church service and support your man. She can't hurt you anymore."

I attended the funeral, even though it was extremely difficult for me to be there, knowing how Steve's mother had felt about me and how the rest of his family still viewed me.

Whenever I had the sense that Steve would never make a long-term commitment to me, he would start making promises. I would tell myself I was being paranoid because I had been hurt in past relationships. What made it all so confusing was that I knew he really loved me. I didn't understand that a person can be in love with you and yet be emotionally unavailable.

When we had been dating for five years, Steve was finally ready to talk about our future. We began making tentative plans. He kept saying he would get a divorce and not doing anything about it. Though I sensed he was wasting my time, he continued to show me a lot of love and we were great together. I thought I just needed to have more patience.

I don't know why I felt the need to get married again. I guess I needed that security, and to know he would not leave me. I had been with him for longer than I had been with Justin, and I needed to know where I was going in life. Deep inside, I knew Steve was not going to commit to me. There were so many red flags, but I kept ignoring them. I should have just walked away and lived my own life instead of waiting for him to be ready to commit, but I was too blinkered.

Sometimes we just don't realize we are being manipulated, as hiding it constitutes part of the manipulation. When I look back on it now, I can see that Steve was doing exactly that. He told me what I wanted to hear. At that time in my life, I did not have the strength or courage to walk away. His family's constant criticism of me had chipped away at my self-esteem. My zest for life, and my confidence, which he'd found so attractive when I met him, were rapidly ebbing away.

We were talking about our engagement, but I knew he had not filed any divorce papers. It is the longest I have ever stayed in a relationship after realizing it was headed nowhere. In the past I had always had the strength to leave. This time around, that strength was nowhere to be found.

Breaking Point

It was summer, and we had been enjoying a spell of fabulous weather. Steve and I were living together at his place, and I had committed to renting out my place for another two years. He had an enormous garden where we loved to while away the balmy evenings. One afternoon, we were relaxing in the garden and chatting about the vacation we were about to take. The following day, we would be heading off to Spain for a week.

Steve's sister was visiting at the time. She came into the garden and started laying into me. She called me a tramp and said I had destroyed their family.

I stood up and said, "That's it! I have had enough of this. Who the hell do you think you are?"

She hurled her glass against the paving stones, and it smashed to smithereens. Some shards hit Bertie and cut his nose. Penny had passed away a few months earlier, so Bertie was my only dog. Seeing that she had hurt him, I went ballistic and slapped her across the face. She started screaming bloody murder.

I said, "All your money hasn't bought you any class. How dare you come here and attack me and my dog!"

I didn't know what to do. Steve told me to go for a walk and he would deal with it. As I walked down to the beach with Bertie, I was in shock and felt petrified about my future. The confrontation had left a bad taste in my mouth. As enraged as I was by the things Steve's sister had said and done, I wasn't surprised or even hurt, as she had already despised the idea of me before she had even met me. What really hurt was seeing the way Steve had just let it happen. Instead of rising to my defense or telling his sister she was being out of order, he had simply stood there.

I thought of how he had rushed me out of the place, saying he would talk to her. He was probably sitting there quietly while she said terrible things about me. Could I spend my life with a man who wouldn't defend me to his own family? If I'd had an ounce of self-respect left at this point, I would have walked away. For the last two years my dad had been telling me to leave but I hadn't had the strength or the self-love to get up and leave, and I certainly didn't have it now. I was so in love, and we were about to go on vacation.

A little later, Steve phoned me and apologized for his sister's behavior. The following day we flew off to Spain as planned. We both acted as if everything was normal and tried to have fun and relax, but things felt strained. Our entire vacation was shrouded in a very strange atmosphere.

After we returned home, I resumed therapy with Clare for a few months. I had stopped seeing her about a year before I met Steve, so it was good to check in with her and talk about everything that had been going on. As always, she helped me to gain a clearer perspective and place everything in context. She encouraged me to be patient with Steve at this time, as he was probably grieving the loss of his mother.

Meanwhile, my relationship with Steve's family was growing ever more tumultuous, and the constant strain was making me feel anxious and depressed. I felt I couldn't keep living this way, but I did not know how to transform the situation. Ideally, we should all have been able to come together, lay everything out on the table, and talk things through, but because his family viewed everything I did in a negative light, I knew if I were to attempt to initiate a discussion, they would think I was instigating trouble or being confrontative. I would never be given a fair chance to explain where I was coming from, and Steve would not advocate for me.

All I could do was to keep trying to fit into their world, to be someone I am not, and to live up to their impossible standards, even though nothing I did would ever satisfy them. It was so frustrating and utterly demoralizing, but I felt I had no choice. My only other option was to walk away, and I wasn't willing to do that. I was so in love with Steve, and I had invested all this time in our relationship. I kept telling myself he would eventually come through on all his promises. Someday things would get easier. I just had to get through this.

The Beginning of the End

One Thursday morning, my dad phoned me and asked me to meet him for coffee in Holywood. I said I would love to. I asked him if everything was OK. He said he wanted to have a chat with me.

When I arrived at the coffee shop, he said he had some bad news. I immediately felt sick. My mind started racing. My dad always played everything down, so I had to read between the lines. He said he'd been having some tests done over the past few months. These had confirmed that he had a tumor in one of his lungs.

I gasped. "What? Why did you not tell me weeks ago?"

"I couldn't," he said. "I knew how much it would upset you, so I didn't want to tell you until I had all the facts."

I said, "Well, what are the facts?"

"I don't know yet. My appointment is tomorrow at the City Hospital, and I don't want to tell your mum."

"I am going with you," I said.

My dad always protected my mum. She would not have been able to deal with such news, as she depended so much on my dad.

"OK," he said. "My appointment is at lunchtime."

I told him I would collect him and bring him to his appointment. As I left that day, I was numb. I didn't know how to digest what I had just been told. My mind was spinning.

What if this is terminal? How will I cope without my dad, who has always been there to talk about everything in my life and guide me?

I rang Steve and told him the news. He suggested going for a walk and having dinner at the Dirty Duck, which was a pub just down the beach.

I said, "That would be great. I am so sad."

That evening, Steve comforted me. He said, "Don't think the worst. It will be OK."

I could not stop worrying. The thought of my dad being seriously ill was so frightening.

The next morning as Steve was getting ready to leave for work, he said, "You're a great daughter, supporting your dad at this time. Ring me when you leave the hospital, OK? I will be thinking about you."

I picked up my dad and we went to the City Hospital to meet the oncologist. He was skinny grey man with absolutely no personality. I could tell my dad was nervous as we sat down at the doctor's desk.

My dad tried to break the tension with a joke. "Doctor," he said, "I've just started reading *War and Peace*—will I have enough time to finish it?"

The doctor looked blankly at him. "You have small cell cancer. The tumor can't be removed, so would you like to know how long you have left?"

I guess these guys break this kind of news to people daily, but I felt he could have shown some empathy. I looked at my dad and saw real fear in his eyes, the likes of which I had never seen before.

"No, thank you," Dad said. "Just tell me my treatment."

I was fighting back tears and didn't want to break down when my dad had enough to deal with, so I excused myself and left the doctor's office.

I went to the bathroom and rang my sister. I was crying.

"It's not good," I said. "I will ring you later."

She started crying, which set me off even more. After ending the call, I pulled myself together and took some deep breaths. I wanted to be strong for my dad. As I re-entered the doctor's office, the doctor was telling my dad that he would be starting chemo the following Monday.

As we left the hospital, I said to my dad, "Let's go to my house and have a nice walk on the beach.

"Yes," Dad said. "That would be nice." Even though he was in shock, he remained calm and pragmatic.

As we drove to my house, he said, "I have had a good life, but I would have liked to have had a little longer."

We walked along the beach and cried.

I said, "I will take you there for every treatment. Who knows what can happen? Sometimes they get it wrong."

He laughed.

When I saw Steve that evening, I was in a trance. "I don't know how to deal with this," I told him.

"You're a strong woman," he said. "You will be fine. Look after your dad. He needs you."

It was a Friday evening. I said, "Can we go to the movies? I need to keep my mind off everything until Monday morning."

"Sure, anything you want," he said. "Let's have dinner first."

We arrived at Deanne's Deli, a lovely restaurant close to the cinema. As we sat down for dinner, I saw some people I knew who happened to be seated at a nearby table. They came over and chatted to us for a while. Steve was his usual quiet self.

Once we were alone again, we talked about my dad.

"I'm so worried about him," I said.

"I know," he said.

My mind was reeling. I kept trying to picture what the future would look like without my dad, but first I would have to get through the next hours, days, and weeks. I couldn't even begin to imagine what they held in store. I wanted to support my dad by accompanying him to every chemo appointment, even though I knew it was going to be hard. It was good to know that Steve would be by my side through it all.

We had talked so much about getting engaged, but I hadn't put any kind of deadline on it. I had just been glad we were getting somewhere, so I'd been willing to bide my time, but learning of my dad's prognosis changed my perspective on this. I didn't know how much time my dad would have left. I hoped that he would live to see my wedding day, but at the very least I wanted my dad to be at my engagement and to know where my life was heading. I was slightly nervous about bringing this up with Steve, but I wanted us to be on the same page.

"Hey," I said, "with my dad not being well, maybe we should get engaged at Christmas."

December was a few months away, and we had already talked so much about getting engaged. It would just be a question of pulling it a bit closer. I wasn't asking for the moon.

Steve blinked at me. "You know, I'm not sure if I'm ready for that kind of commitment. I'm not sure if I want to get married again."

My stomach turned. I wanted to scream. "What are you talking about? We've been discussing this for the past year."

"I know," he said, "but my daughter is never going to accept you, and I just can't deal with the conflict anymore. It would be best if you move out."

The whole room started spinning like a cyclone, with me in the center. This couldn't be happening. Just then, the waiter arrived with our food. My acquaintances at the next table were looking at us. The tension was so thick you could have cut it with a knife, and our body language said it all.

I stood up. "I need to get out of here."

I picked up my handbag, walked out of the restaurant and stood on the sidewalk wondering what had just happened. Could this be real? I couldn't feel anything. Was I dreaming?

Steve emerged from the restaurant, having settled the bill. I just stared at him.

I have been with this man for six years, I thought. *For all this time I have been asking him if he can really picture a future with me. He could have chosen any day to tell me the truth. Why now?*

"I want to go home," I said.

We got into a taxi and rode home in silence. I was in shock. It had been three days since I discovered my dad had cancer; two days since I learned I was going to lose him; and one hour since I found out my boyfriend was not only breaking up with me, but he was also kicking me out.

When we pulled up in front of the house, I ran inside, closed the front door, doubled over, and began to howl. My emotions unleashed and everything came pouring out. The pain was indescribable. I cried so hard I thought I was going to break a rib. Steve came into the house and stood there watching me, an impassive look on his face.

When I had calmed down enough to speak, I said, "What am I going to do? Where am I supposed to go?"

Steve stared blankly at me.

"My house has been rented out for the next two years," I sobbed. "I can't go live in a hotel—I have a dog, and a business I run from home."

Steve's expression remained ice-cold and emotionless as he spoke. "You have enough friends. You can stay with one of them until you find a place to live."

I became hysterical. I grabbed him and said, "How can you say this to me?"

"It's just not there," he said. "I don't love you enough."

When I heard those words come out of his mouth, I wanted to die. My heart was destroyed. What hurt the most—much more than finding out he didn't want me in his life—was his sheer indifference to my pain. The complete absence of kindness and warmth. In that moment, I really needed him to be a friend. I just wanted him to show me a glimpse of the person I knew, but he remained distant and unfeeling. I could not come to terms with his coldness, his complete detachment.

"How can you do this to me?" I asked him. "How can you be so cold? How can you love someone for six years and then, the moment you decide it's over, suddenly stop caring about them? I don't understand.

How do you expect me to pack up my life right now, and go and sleep on someone's sofa? I'm taking my dad to chemo on Monday."

He said he was sorry about the timing, but that it was what he wanted. "There is no good time," he said.

I wanted to kill him. I wanted him to suffer as much as I was suffering right then. I told myself that if I were to harm him, I would end up in jail, and then my life really would be over. I plunged into a bottomless pit of despair. My heart was physically aching, and I couldn't do anything to make it stop.

"Go to sleep," Steve said. "Leave me alone." He went into his son's bedroom and locked the door.

I stood there, frozen. When we left for dinner, we were a couple. We'd had dreams, a future. We were in love. I could never have imagined we would be coming home to this. I went and found Bertie, my collie.

"Bertie, what am I going to do? How am I going to cope?"

I went to bed, in what used to be our bedroom. Bertie climbed in with me, and I hugged him all night.

In the morning, my eyes were so swollen I could hardly see. I felt like a zombie. I went out into the hall and saw that Steve had already left. I rang his cellphone, and he didn't answer.

I phoned Kathy, who lived down the beach. When I told her what had happened, she was so shocked.

"Come over," she said.

Bertie and I walked to her house. I could not stop crying. Kathy helped me talk things through and try to figure out what to do. I remembered that my friend Laura had a house nearby that stood unoccupied at the time. I phoned Laura and explained my situation. She was very empathetic.

I asked her whether she would let me stay in her vacant house while I figured out where to go.

"Of course you can," Laura said.

My angel. I was so grateful.

I left Kathy's place and spent the rest of the day walking Bertie on the beach in a trance-like state. I sat on the sand and looked at the sea.

Please, God—why are You doing this to me? What have I done to deserve this?

Is it me? Am I doomed? Am I not allowed to be happy?

I love this man more than I ever loved anyone, and I am losing him.

As the sun began to set, I knew I had to pull myself together. In the morning, I would be bringing my dad to the hospital for his first chemotherapy session.

I went home, and there was still no sign of Steve. I went to bed and cuddled Bertie.

The following day, I collected my dad. I tried to act normal and upbeat although I felt like I was living in a nightmare. We arrived at the hospital and chatted with the doctor. I sat there listening to them talk but not really taking anything in.

When we went into the waiting area, my dad said, "What's wrong?"

"Nothing," I said.

"Don't lie," my dad said.

I guess our parents know us better than we think they do.

"It's fine," I said. "You have enough to deal with right now. I'm OK."

"What is it?"

I took a deep breath. "Steve and I—"

My dad cut me off. "Please don't tell me he is doing this to you now."

"Yes," I said, bursting into tears.

"What a total bastard," Dad said. He rarely cursed. He hugged me and said, "I am so, so sorry, Denise. I always felt he would do this to you. He was never going to marry you. In his eyes and in the eyes of his family, you were never good enough. They will never forget you are Catholic."

I said, "I'm heartbroken. How can I cope with another failure?"

"It's OK. There is someone out there who's right for you, and who deserves your love. And he will find you, I promise."

Then my dad was called in, and I had to leave. I told him I would come back in three hours to collect him.

As I left the hospital, I had that feeling again, like I wanted to drive my car into a hedge and never wake up. I was crying so much I couldn't see the road in front of me. I didn't know how things would ever get better.

Just then, Steve texted me to say he was going to the UK on business for three days. The implication was that I should move out of the house before he returned. I didn't need to be asked twice. He didn't ask about how things were going with my dad. How had I spent six years in a relationship with a person who had no empathy?

I phoned my friends Sonia and Bernard and told them what was happening. They said they would help me with the move. They had a horse box, so we would be able to do it in a few runs. Most of my furniture was still in my own house, which I had rented out, but I had stored a few pieces in Steve's garage. I would be able to use them in Laura's house to make it feel less empty.

I moved out of Steve's house five days after he told me it was over. I did not want to be made to feel unwelcome in a place I had once called home. All my friends came down and helped me to pack my belongings. Even my wee dad wanted to help, even though he had just undergone his first chemo session. My heart broke every time I looked at him. I wanted to kill Steve for doing this to me just when my dad needed me most.

Dark Days

On my first night in Laura's vacant house, when everyone had left, it was just me, my mum, and Bertie. We closed the front door and looked around. It was an enormous, detached house with eight bedrooms. There was no heating yet.

My mum gave me a hug and said, "You're so brave."

What choice did I have? I would have to try to pick up the pieces of my life. I was so sad that night. I really couldn't understand how a person who had once loved me could treat me so badly, especially when I had just found out my dad was leaving this world.

I texted Steve a few times. He didn't reply, which made me feel even worse.

The next morning, I woke up in a cold house and had a cold shower. As the icy water streamed down my body, I stood there crying and feeling lost.

How will I get through this? I asked myself. *How can I live in this huge house alone?*

I knew I would be able to find love again, but I didn't want to start over.

In the weeks following, it was a struggle to get through each day. I would sleep until noon and wake up feeling exhausted. On the days when I wasn't taking my dad to chemo, I could hardly get out of bed.

I asked Laura whether I could stay for a month while I figured things out.

She said, "You can stay as long as you want."

It was so kind of Laura to let me move in at such short notice. Later, she said I could stay in her house until my tenants moved out of my house, so instead of staying for one month, I would end up staying there for two years. Her house was such a nice place for me to live while I was healing from the breakup and dealing with the impending loss of my dad. She charged me less rent than she could have, and I counted myself very fortunate to have this beautiful place in which to recover.

The house overlooked the sea and had an amazing view. After each of my dad's chemo treatments, we would come back and sit by the window looking out at the ocean and chatting about life.

One afternoon, he turned to me and said, "Always remember to appreciate nature. Stop and take the time to look at the birds, the flowers, and the sea. It isn't until we are leaving this world that we realize how important they are. All too often, we don't even see the beauty all around us."

I will never forget that. I cherished every moment we spent together in those last months. He knew how badly I was hurting during this time, even though I did my best not to show it. I wanted to be strong for him and for myself, but I was starting to feel like giving up.

What lies ahead? I often wondered. *How can I rebuild my life?*

In early October, when I had been living in Laura's house for about three weeks, I was walking along the beach and enjoying the autumn sunshine when I received a call from Spencer. He's one of my suppliers, and we had become good friends.

"Are you sitting down?" he said.

"No, I am outside walking around," I said.

"Well," he said, "I have just found out that Steve is dating my ex-wife. I thought you might want to know."

"No," I said. "That can't be right."

I knew Spencer's ex-wife, Carol. She had befriended me a few months ago. I had invited her along sometimes when Steve and I went out.

"He picked her up last night," Spencer said. "I watched her get into his car."

"I feel sick," I said. "Sorry. I'll call you back."

I ended the call and threw up on the sand. Then I phoned Steve.

"Is it true?" I demanded. "Are you seeing Carol?"

"Yes," he said. "And it has nothing to do with you. It's over between us, and you need to accept that and move on."

"It's been three weeks!" I screamed. "This is my friend—she *was* my friend! How can you do this to me?"

Steve hung up on me.

I wanted to die. It was bad enough getting dumped in such a callous manner. To think he was having sex with one of my friends made me sick to my stomach. Crying, I phoned my dad. He told me to come home.

I drove to my parents' house.

"How can he do this?" I asked my dad. "Doesn't he know how much this is hurting me?"

"He has no emotion towards you," Dad said. "He probably moved on long before he ended things with you. Anyway, this woman will fit into the life his family wants for him."

I knew he was right. Carol is Protestant and went to a private school. Steve's family would adore her. I began to wonder whether I had missed something. Did Carol befriend me just to get close to him? Had this all been going on right in front of my eyes?

"Do you think he was seeing her behind my back?" I asked my dad.

He looked sadly at me. "I don't know."

"At least Justin's mistress was in Bulgaria, so I'll never have to see her, but I am probably going to bump into these two all the time. How will I cope? What if I say or do something I will regret?"

In my dad's eyes, I could see that he knew how much pain I was in, and that he wished he could make it better. I felt terrible that I was burdening him with my problems when he was already suffering. I hugged my parents and drove home.

A few weeks later, I walked into the local coffee shop. When I saw Carol sitting there, I froze in my tracks. She had the nerve to say hello to me. I wanted to slap her, but I wasn't about to lose my dignity in front of this woman I had once considered my friend.

I turned and walked back out. I got in my car and bawled my eyes out.

What is going on in my life? I thought. *When did everybody stop being human?*

About a month later, a good friend, who also lived in Holywood, told me he had run into Steve and Carol the previous night. They had told him it was their first night out in public as a couple, and that I really needed to move on. I am sure my friend believed it was the right thing to tell me, but I wished he hadn't.

That night, I drank two bottles of wine. I went down to the seashore and wept. I contemplated walking in and letting the ocean take me.

I kept telling myself, *Just do it, come on, do it.*

I just didn't have the balls. I felt like my life was over anyway, and I didn't want to be here anymore. Life on earth was proving to be too painful. My emotional resources were thoroughly depleted. I had nothing left inside me to bring me back from this heartbreak. It felt like I was not allowed to be happy, because every time I found love, it was taken away from me.

I phoned Clare and said, "Can I start seeing you again?"

"Of course," she said. "Come over straight away."

I didn't know if therapy would help me, but I knew I had to give it a try. Clare was sad to hear what had happened. She had been Steve's therapist after I recommended seeing her, so she knew him, and she knew his character. She had thought we were great together and hadn't seen this coming, either.

While all this was going on, my mum phoned me in tears. She was so upset. She said my dad's hair was falling out in the shower. When I heard this, I just started sobbing. It was all too much to take. I felt like my whole world was caving in.

That winter I was drinking more than usual. I had a group of new friends that would regularly come over to the house. I loved to party with them, and I needed an excuse to drink, as this was my only coping mechanism. I was trying to heal my heartache by self-medicating with alcohol, but it only numbed the pain and only temporarily. I would wake up the next morning with a hangover, and my heart would still ache just as badly.

During this time, I wasn't focused on my work. I dealt only with what was required of me day to day. Due to company buyouts, I had lost some accounts. I needed to seek out new business but had no desire to do so. I had lost my drive, and my self-esteem had plummeted. I had lost a lot of weight because I was so disconnected from my body and my needs. My stomach was always in knots, and I had no appetite.

At Christmas, I prepared the festive lunch for my sister, my mum, and my dad. It was the first Christmas in six years I had spent without Steve. The house, with its stunning views, looked exquisite. I had decorated it beautifully for the occasion and lit the large open fire. It was so cozy, and the perfect setting for my dad's last Christmas with us.

I began the new year feeling extremely low. Dealing with all this emotion was taking its toll. I didn't want to work. I didn't want to get up. All I wanted to do was to take my dad to hospital, and to party with my friends. I couldn't plan any holidays, as I didn't know how much time my dad had left. I wanted to be there for him.

I had met a lovely guy while I was out with my friends around Christmas. His name was Conor, and he had a fun personality and a cheeky attitude. We had kept in touch and gone on a few dates, but I found myself still missing Steve. I wished it could be him looking at me from across the table. I liked hanging out with Conor, but this was all I really wanted from him at the time.

I started going more frequently to Dublin for nights out. A group of us would head up there on a Saturday to party. We would often go to

House, a club on Leeson Street, then spend the night in Dublin and head home on the Sunday. I loved it so much. Being there took my mind off everything I was dealing with at that time. But when I returned home on Sunday, it would all come rushing back, like a tidal wave.

My weekend trips to Dublin had become a little escape for me. On one of these weekends, my friend Katrina brought along a friend with whom I instantly clicked. She was attractive, fun, and exciting—just what I needed to help take my mind off everything I had lost. We became great friends, and she spent most of that year staying with me at the large house. She was footloose and fancy-free, and she enjoyed spending time with me. I needed some company, and she came along at the right time.

The Bright Side

My dad's condition gradually worsened over the next months, but he would never complain to us. One Sunday afternoon, about ten months since he had been diagnosed, he was having difficulty breathing. We rang for an ambulance to take him to hospital.

After he was admitted, a doctor come and spoke to us. "He is very unwell and should have been in hospital before now. He didn't let you know that he was struggling because he hadn't wanted to upset you or cause you to worry. He wanted life to remain close to normal for as long as possible."

For my mum, who had been in denial about his illness, this news came as a bombshell. She was very dependent upon my dad, so both he and I had tried to shield her from the reality that he was going to die.

The doctor said, "He is a remarkable man, and you should all be very proud of him." She was crying. I will never forget that.

Four days later, my dad passed away. We were all gathered around him praying the rosary. I had never lost anyone that close to me before, and I was devastated when he took his last breath, but I am grateful that I could look after him in his last months, that we could share that time together driving to all his hospital visits, and that I was able to tell him I loved him moments before he passed away. My dad made sure that we could all say goodbye to him before he left this world. He was a selfless man who always put everyone else's needs first, even on his deathbed.

I told my family I would look after the funeral arrangements. I wanted to take care of this, as he had told me exactly what he wanted. I was determined to carry out his wishes.

My mum was grief-stricken by my dad's death, and she was taking it out on me. She refused to speak to me to that day, and for many days afterward. Although I understood that this was caused by her undiagnosed psychological issues, it was very hard to take. Above all, I felt it was sad that we couldn't console each other, just when we needed each other the most.

On my way home that evening, I drove past Steve and Carol. They were holding hands and laughing as they walked along the street. It required all my self-control to resist the temptation to run them over with my car. This had been the darkest day of my life and I was about to go into a huge, empty house to seek comfort from my dog and a glass of wine. The last thing I needed right now was to see Steve prancing around.

Never in my life had I felt so alone and so empty. But I didn't want any friends around me. I needed to be by myself. I needed time to process what had just happened. I had lost my dad, who I went to for everything. How was I going to face life without him?

The next day, I set about making funeral arrangements and writing the eulogy. I spent all day working on it. I wanted to get it right, and I had so much I wanted to say. I didn't even know how I would be able to deliver it, but I was determined to do it in my father's honor.

On the day of the funeral, my mum still wasn't talking to me. It was hard enough facing up to the loss of my dad. It was incredibly difficult but having to deal with her issues as well. I really needed her to give me a hug.

The funeral was a beautiful tribute to my dad. Many of his friends and colleagues got up and spoke about him and what a great and humble man he was. I managed to deliver the entire eulogy without crying. I could feel my dad's love giving me the strength to finish it. He had told me he wanted the Monty Python song "Always Look on the Bright Side of Life" to be played as his coffin was lowered. There wasn't a dry eye in the place. It was the perfect send-off.

In the days after the funeral, I kept thinking Steve would send his condolences via a letter or a text. He never did. This really hurt, especially when I remembered how I had been there for him after his mother's death. Justin had come to the hospital many times to support me, and both David and Justin had attended my dad's funeral. The fact that Steve couldn't even be bothered to send a sympathy note made me think he lacked all human emotions. How could he be so cold?

Why did I stay with him? Why didn't I just run off with Lyndsay? I could not turn back the clock. I had allowed a man to destroy my sense of self and leave me with my life and my heart in tatters. I can never forgive him for how he treated me. If I ever pass him on the street, I will just keep walking.

Aftermath

My dad's death left me with such a feeling of emptiness. My heart ached. The pain was indescribable.

A friend said, "Why don't you go and see this emotional healing person?"

"OK, give me the number," I said.

I was willing to try anything at this stage. I called them up and made an appointment to see them.

About a week after my dad's funeral, my collie, Bertie, got sick. I took him to the vet, and he had to stay there for three days. I was on tenterhooks.

Please, please, please, I prayed. *Don't take him away from me.*

The day Bertie was allowed to come home, I rushed to the vet's office to pick him up. He was glad to see me, though he seemed a little dazed. I showered him with gentle kisses, brought him home, and got him settled in. A few hours later, he passed away.

I've heard it said that dogs have a sixth sense, and Bertie was exceptionally smart and perceptive. He had loved my dad and would follow him around whenever he visited. I believe Bertie knew how much I needed him, so he made sure he stayed with me until after my dad died.

A few days later I was sitting on my bed, having cried my eyes out for the zillionth time. My heart ached, and my eyes were so swollen that it hurt to blink. I felt like a zombie. I missed my dad and I missed Bertie. I even missed Steve. Everyone was gone. What was the point in living? I rang my friend and told her I needed help.

She said, "Sweetheart, I know. Will you please call your doctor as soon as we hang up?"

"Yes," I said. "Thank you."

I rang my GP.

"Dear, oh dear," he said. "Why did you not ring me sooner?"

"I thought I could handle it by myself," I said. "I thought it would get better."

"Dear, you can't cope with all this loss alone. It is too great. I will prescribe you a light antidepressant."

"OK," I said. I was not keen on taking medication, but I knew I needed help.

I then attended a day retreat with the emotional healing person. Like me, the other people in attendance had suffered losses and wanted to heal from them. Many hoped to connect with the spirit world. It was a very special day that I will never forget. We all wore white. As soon as the relaxing meditation music began to play, I started to cry, and I could not stop. Floods of tears just kept pouring out. I felt like I was letting go of everything.

After the day retreat, I arranged a one-to-one session with the healer. She helped me to understand why so many things had been happening to me at once. She said that sometimes things happen this way, and it is part of our journey. She said she could feel I am highly intuitive and sensitive, and this is a skill I might wish to explore further. She told me that the little girl within me needs to heal before I can move forward. Everything she said to me made a lot of sense, but at the time I was so torn up by grief that I just wanted someone to press a button and fix my heart.

In addition to the stress of adjusting to life without my dad and without Bertie, I was worried about my finances. Pretty much throughout my six-year relationship with Steve, I had been living beyond my means. In my efforts to keep up with him and to earn his family's acceptance, I had often contributed more to our household and holiday expenses than I could reasonably afford. I had ended up dipping into my savings and my business capital to make ends meet.

I kept telling myself that a more prosperous time lay right around the corner, that soon we would have less relationship stress and I would be able to fully devote myself to work, but that time had never come. Instead, my world had imploded: I had been blindsided by the news of my dad's terminal illness, and then Steve had unceremoniously dumped me and thrown me out of the house. Over the past year I had been in survival mode and had not been working at my usual capacity. Things were now starting to get tight for me, financially speaking, and this sense of economic uncertainty compounded the loss of the emotional safety I had once had with my dad, my dog, and my boyfriend.

A few months after my dad died, Steve and Carol got married. I was devastated by the news.

My so-called friends eagerly phoned me up. "Have you seen the photos in the magazine?" they chirped.

I wanted to go over to their houses and thump them. How inconsiderate can people be? I don't know if they were really that clueless or whether they were secretly gloating over my misfortune. Either way, I was stunned by their lack of empathy. I decided that as soon as my tenants moved out, I would sell the house and move away. This was the only way I would be able to move on. I could not deal with constantly having this marriage rubbed in my face.

Selling my house would give me all my equity back, and I would be able to start over in a new location. As time went on, I continued to struggle. I was not coping at all, and I was still self-medicating with alcohol even though I was now on medication. It was a bad combination, and I often became very angry and wanted to pick a fight. I had been advised not to drink while on antidepressants but giving up alcohol wasn't really an option during this time.

The day finally came when my tenants moved out and I got my house back. I was planning to stay there until I sold it, so I started cleaning it and preparing to move back in. I had it surveyed to find out what it was currently worth. What I learned next came as an enormous blow. The value of my house was diminishing. It was no longer mortgageable, and it was valued as a cash sale only.

God, I said, *why are you punishing me? Haven't I suffered enough for one lifetime?* My home was not even worth what was on the mortgage, and I had lost all my equity, which should have been between £250K and £300K.

It was humiliating. I was forty-seven and having to rethink my entire life. I had spent all my money; my business was under serious pressure; the house had to go; and I was going to lose all my equity, in addition to everything else I had lost. I had reached my limit.

"That's it," I said. "I am done. I can't go on."

Then, I picked up the pieces and carried on living. First, I had to walk away from my beloved home. I decided to rent a small house in Holywood, where I could live while I figured out what I was going to do. My business had diminished, and I simply didn't have the confidence to try and sell to people. I could not even bring myself to pick up the phone to ask for a meeting. It was simply too daunting. My fear of rejection was too great.

I had always known that Justin would be there for me if I ever needed him, and he was. When I lost the house, he gave me a lot of guidance. He also tried to get me to take him back.

"Justin," I said, "I am suffering. I am still emotionally connected to Steve, and I can't just move on. I will always care for you, but I think we are done romantically. Too much has happened."

No matter what happened between Justin and me, at least he always wanted to try and make things better. Steve, on the other hand, had no empathy or respect for me or my dad. For that, I will never forgive him.

During this time, I found out who my real friends are. A few of my friends stood by me and supported me through it all, and we remain close to this day. I am grateful for all they did for me. Without them, I don't know how I would have survived this stretch of my life.

Many of my friends felt they needed to distance themselves from me because they disapproved of the way I was dealing with my pain. They had been happy to stick around while our friendship benefited them, but right when I needed their compassion and empathy, they ditched me. They would hang out with Steve and Carol in the local bar, shrieking with laughter and acting all matey with them, while I stood at the other end of the bar feeling worthless and alone. To this day, I wonder where I got the strength to stay in the bar on those evenings and to withstand the pain they inflicted upon me. Sometimes I think I was numb to a lot of it.

When I look back at the girls who judged me and abandoned our friendship, I wonder: if life had thrown all those things at them, instead of at me, how would *they* have dealt with it?

A New Leaf

I moved into a lovely little place on the seafront, a bit closer to the village. My good friend, who owned a local estate agency, had helped me to secure it. I had been missing Bertie and needed another furry friend to comfort me, so I adopted a black cocker spaniel from the rescue home and named her Zara. She was a cuddly little teddy bear who needed a lot of love and attention, because her previous owner was abusive.

I started developing a new business concept. Men were always asking me to recommend gift ideas for their wives or their mums, so I wanted to set up a shopping concierge service. I have always been good at choosing gifts and clothes for other people, so I knew I could make this work. I started investing money into my business model, which I called Shop Brownie Points, as the person who gave the gift would receive the Brownie points for the gift I had chosen on their behalf.

At this point I no longer had enough print clients to attain my desired sales volume. Looking back, I can see I may have been relying too heavily on social media to generate leads. I had rented a desk at my friend's PR company in the hopes that going into an office every day would inspire me to shoot for the stars, but I was still not hitting my monthly targets, and I was spending copious amounts of money trying to make it work.

I felt that if I wanted my new business to succeed, Dublin was the place for me. I joined two networking groups—the Dublin Chamber of Business, and Women in Business—and started traveling to Dublin every other week to promote my new business and forge new connections there. Zara hated being away from me, so I would often drive to Dublin so I could bring her with me in the car.

I loved these trips to Dublin, but on the return journey I always felt like I was entering a dark cloud. For me, Holywood had come to represent so many painful memories and so much negative energy.

At the networking events, I met many bright, successful, and empowered women and established some beautiful friendships. I became fast friends with a businesswoman named Treasa, who said that Zara and I would be welcome to stay with her whenever I came to Dublin.

That summer Treasa offered me her house for a full week, so Zara and I packed our bags and headed to Dublin for our holidays. I loved my time in Castleknock, which is on the north side of Dublin. Treasa's house was right on the canal, so Zara and I would often stroll alongside it and visit Phoenix Park. Phoenix Park is the largest park in Europe. I had gone there to see Pope John Paul II back in 1979. Zara and I would go out there with a picnic lunch and lie on the grass relaxing and watching deer. The park is full of beautiful deer. I loved to see them roaming freely.

Whenever I came to Dublin, I felt like a new person. I sensed that the city held so much potential for me. I wondered why I had not started spending time there years ago. Why did I always fall into relationships, instead of living life as I wanted? I'd always had a huge love for Dublin.

My friends would often say, "Denise, you love that Dublin!"

I had always wanted to live in Dublin but had never had the courage to move there. Now I was down there all the time, which was the next best thing.

I loved making new friends who didn't know what I had suffered through or to whom I had been married. They accepted me and liked me just as I was. I started to believe that people could love me for being myself. I learned to stop obsessing over my social status and material wealth, and to start valuing my inner qualities instead.

After I had spent a year living between Holywood and Dublin, driving up and down, I was faced with a decision. My business was failing, so I needed to find a job. All I had ever known was print, and I wanted out of it.

By autumn, I was feeling good about myself again, though my financial concerns were always lurking at the back of my mind. I was loving my nights out in the city and had been getting attention from men again. I was invited to appear on First Dates Ireland. I thought, *Why the hell not? It will be good fun and help my confidence.* We filmed the episode in late September, and it would air on RTE in early January.

In December, I was in Dublin to attend the Dublin Chamber Christmas Lunch and would be spending the night in the city. My friend Wendy and I got all dressed up and we both looked a million dollars. Wendy was a lovely new friend. She has a fun and bubbly personality, and we had just clicked from the first time we met. We had a wonderful time that night. At the end of the evening, a man from the Chamber approached me. We had chatted quite a few times that day.

"You're a firecracker," he said, "and I would like to discuss a job offer with you."

I was delighted. It was as though the Universe had sent him to me.

We met up the following day and he offered me a job. I accepted it on the spot.

I rang Wendy and said, "Guess what? I'm moving to Dublin! And I have a new job starting in January."

She screamed with excitement. "When in January?" she asked.

"The sixth!"

She screamed again. "That's so soon!" she yelped.

"Yes, it is!" I yelped back. It was the eighth of December. "Oh my God, I have less than a month to sort everything out! I better start finding a place to live."

I logged into the Daft app and started searching through homes to rent. I already knew I wanted to live in Dún Laoghaire. I had fallen in love with it the year before, while visiting my friend Richard. I found an apartment right across from the beautiful People's Park and close to the pier. I couldn't believe my luck. It was the perfect place and location.

When I went to view the apartment, I remember walking in and thinking it might be too small. It had one small bedroom and a tiny kitchen, but it had a garden and a fireplace, and I loved the location. I told the landlord I would take it. I made a video of the apartment. It was unfurnished, so I would need to work out which of my furniture to keep and which to sell.

The landlord said, "There are others coming to view it, so I will let you know."

I rang him every day for the next week.

Finally, he said, "The place is yours."

I was so excited to make a new start in life. I simply could not stay in Holywood for another minute. All its ghosts were strangling me, and this was my chance to free myself and move forward. For the first time in a long time, I was happy.

I looked up and said, "Thank you, Dad, for helping me."

I had a few weeks to sell off all my belongings, as there wouldn't be enough room for them in my new apartment and I needed to raise money for the move. I sold the smaller items at car boot sales, and I held a house clearance sale to offload all my beautiful furniture and designer dresses, bags, and shoes. I felt no sadness about letting them go. These items had borne witness to the darkest days of my life, so it felt wonderful to rid myself of them, like a snake shedding its skin. Maybe now some good luck would come my way.

I made around £3K, which covered my deposit and the first month's rent in the new apartment. I kept only what I knew would fit inside my new place and gave the rest to my local charity shop. I had reached the end of the road. I had no choice but to start again.

And this is where we come full circle, to that bright and breezy Dún Laoghaire morning in 2018, when I found myself standing in my new home by the sea. Now you know all about the wild winds that had carried me to this place. I had loved and lost, many times over. I had weathered many storms, and now I could smell the ocean and feel the sun on my face. My father was dead, and my mother had not spoken to me since the day he died. A new chapter in my life was about to unfold. This time I would have only myself, Zara, and my friends to rely on, but I was ready to turn the page.

Debut

Two weeks after I moved to Dún Laoghaire, RTE aired my episode of First Dates Ireland. It felt weird to be appearing on national television when I had recently moved to a new area where I knew almost no-one. Wendy and another girlfriend came over to my place to watch my television debut. I had lit the fire and set out wine and nibbles, and my apartment was feeling so cozy. Zara was cuddled up in front of the fire, ready to watch her mummy appear on television.

I was excited about seeing myself on TV, but I was also anxious about how I would come across. I knew that the way the production company edited the footage might play up certain aspects of my character or storyline. I had just been myself, which is all anyone can do, but how I would be represented was ultimately out of my control. Seeing myself onscreen made me cringe at first. Once I could tell that my bubbly personality was coming across, I started to relax and enjoy the show.

I had been set up with a man who was nice, though he wasn't my type, but we'd had a great time on our date. My date ordered oysters. He had never eaten them before, and they are an acquired taste, so he ended up spitting them out on national television, not once, but twice. I felt sorry for him, but he was very good-natured about it. I laughed along with him, as I didn't want him to feel any worse than he already did. I will never look at oysters the same way again.

It was a fun episode, and I was glad I had agreed to appear on the show. David had always told me I should be on TV, and he may have been right. Perhaps this is something I missed out on in life. I think I could have been a great presenter.

By this time, I had settled into my Dublin life and was enjoying every minute of it. I had always loved going out in Dublin, and now it was right on my doorstep. I was like a kid in a candy store. I attended all kinds of networking events and developed new friendships. I had even started to tentatively dip into the dating pool. Every weekend I was out and about, discovering new places and having a grand time. Strangers would approach me, saying, "Hey, you were on First Dates, weren't you? You were great!"

That made me feel brilliant. I felt like a new woman. I was free of my past, free to be whomever I wanted. No one knew anything about my life leading up to this point, so I felt brand new.

I arrive in the Capital - January 2018

Snowed In

I am not sure whether you recall the Beast from the East arriving in Ireland, but it started at the end of February, a crazy snowstorm that had us all snowed in for four days. Having landed in Dún Laoghaire only seven weeks earlier, I hardly knew anyone, so it was just Zara, me, Netflix, and the fire. Thankfully, the local shop was open, so I ventured there daily for wood and wine supplies. If there is wine and a fire, life is good, right?

    Still, those four days were very lonely, and I thought it would be nice to spend them with a nice man. This started me thinking about how difficult it had been to start dating again, at my age, having been single for three years. I had been considering starting a blog about my journey to Dublin. I wanted to write honestly about the loss I had experienced, in the hopes that my story would encourage other people to believe we can start our lives anew, even after a marriage ends in heartache. We need only to break through our fears. I also wanted to share my stories about various crazy dates I had been on, the fun dates, and the headcases I had encountered.

During that seemingly endless snowstorm, alone by the fireplace, I set up my blog. I decided to call it *Dee's Dublin Life*. From there, it all seemed to happen naturally. I just started sharing stories and videos, in which I talked about my dates in a lighthearted manner. The blog soon became very popular, as so many women related to my experiences. This was when my life in the capital really began. As the blog's readership grew, I was offered lots of interesting opportunities and made many new friends.

I was settling in at my new job, which involved traveling around Ireland. I loved visiting Cork, Galway, and other places in Ireland that had seemed too far away to go for just the weekend when I had lived in Belfast. It had always seemed easier to get a flight to Spain. Seeing so much of my own country was a new adventure. I had less money than I used to have, but I was still able to travel and see so much. I was much happier and that was what really mattered. I truly was living my best life.

During that first year in Dublin, my friends supported me in every way. My lifelong friend, Andrea, often came to visit me bearing practical gifts. She is one of the kindest and most thoughtful people I have ever known.

When I was going through my most trying time before leaving Holywood, she said, "Any friends that left you were never your real friends. No matter what happens, I love you and I always will."

She is a true friend.

Beverly, with whom I had traveled to Marbella and Dublin all those times, is another close ally. She has always had my back. These friends, along with many others, have been my rock.

Conor, who I had met the previous Christmas and had briefly dated, became a close friend. At Easter we went to Galway together, and he later became my accountant. We remain great friends to this day.

Meanwhile, my blog's readership continued to grow. A year after starting my blog, I appeared as a guest on *Dermot & Dave*, a talk show on Today FM, speaking about dating and relationships. This exposure gained me many more subscribers. I was receiving a lot of messages from people who related to the experiences I blogged about and who were having a similar experience in the dating world. It was wonderful to know that my words were resonating with so many people.

I loved working on my blog. Composing a motivational post each day gave my life purpose and direction. I felt fortunate to have a community I could connect with daily, and I valued the sense of companionship, particularly as I knew only a handful of people in my new surroundings at the time. Every day I would get up and post an inspirational quote or record a vlog, in which I spoke candidly about my dating experiences. I started to realize that by posting about my experiences I was helping other people to be the best version of themselves, and this was also helping me.

Sometimes I would post about my nights out in the city with the new friends I had made. Through a networking initiative called Peer to Pier, I made a friend who happened to live just up the road from me. She invited me to an event in the local bar, where I made some new friends in my area. That same night, I got chatting to a blond man who lived just up the road from me.

He said, "I have seen you walking on the pier with your little dog."

"Really?" I said. "Next time, say hello."

The next morning, I awoke with a hangover. Zara was demanding a walk, so I got up and put on the same white jeans and top I had worn the night before. As we headed off down the pier, I spotted Nigel, the man I had met the previous night, bouncing towards me. He had white-blond hair that perfectly matched the fur of his dog, an English

Cream Golden Retriever. They looked so cute together. They stopped, and he chatted to me.

I said, "Sorry, I am still in the same clothes."

He laughed and said, "Yes, I can see that."

He introduced me to Jovi, his gorgeous dog. Zara, ever the small spoilt rascal, wanted to eat the ass off her. From that day, Nigel and I became great friends. We discussed our dating dilemmas, as he too was single and looking for the right partner.

I was beginning to really feel at home. I invited people to join me at various events around the city. Before long, I had established a close circle of likeminded women who loved to have fun and happened to be single. Every weekend we had a plan for where to go. I was so excited every time I went out into the city. For me, it was a dream come true. I had always wanted to live here, and I was living in one of the best parts of South County Dublin.

On many occasions, I would leave House on Leeson Street at around three or four o'clock in the morning and walk along the seafront thinking, *How lucky am I to be here? I have suffered through so much that at times I even considered ending my life, but I'm so happy I never gave up. I have so much to see here and so many people to meet. Imagine if I wasn't here, experiencing all of this.*

Things always get better, though sometimes it takes longer than we expect. Sometimes we are dealt many challenges all at once, but it is possible to move forward.

One evening, at a networking event, a lovely man called Mervyn Greene approached me. He is a very successful businessman who owns the CHQ building, the home of EPIC, The Irish Emigration Museum, in Dublin's Docklands.

Mervyn said, "I have an idea, and I would like to run it by you."

I said, "Give me a call anytime. I'd love to hear more about it."

I was intrigued and excited to know what he had planned.

A few days later, he phoned me. He said he wanted to set a new Guinness World Record by organizing the world's largest speed dating event. It would take place in his building on Valentine's Day, and he wanted me to host it. The record to beat had been set in Calgary, Canada, in 2014.

I told him I would love to do it. I was excited and quite bowled over that he had chosen me to be the face of this amazing event.

Mervyn said, "You will be promoting it on every radio station we can get you on."

He was extremely well connected, so I knew this was going to be amazeballs. Here I was, a little blow-in. Within a year of arriving in Dublin I had been on TV and now little old me, from Antrim, was being asked to host this big event. I felt on top of the world. It occurred to me that all the best things seemed to happen whenever I was going it alone, without a man by my side.

I put all my energy into promoting the event. I bought myself a bright pink dress and arranged to get a blowout and have my makeup professionally done before the event. A thousand attendees showed up on the night. Of these, 964 people participated. As well as raising money for Movember Ireland and Breast Cancer Awareness, we succeeded in setting a new world record. At the time of writing, this record still stands.

Mervyn could not have known how happy he had made me by asking me to host this event. His belief in me helped boost my confidence and self-esteem. So many good things were happening for me. These opportunities had come my way only because I had pushed myself, in setting up my blog, appearing on First Dates, and attending every networking event I could find.

I believe that nothing comes to you for free. If you want opportunities, you must take risks and work hard to ensure those risks will pay off. Starting my own business had required me to take a leap of faith, as had moving to Dublin. I had no idea if I would fit in or what the journey was going to be like, but I took the risk and as a result I was now happier than I ever thought I would be.

I felt excited and hopeful about the future, even though I was struggling to make ends meet. In Dublin the cost of living is greater than it is in Belfast. I was paying €1,350 a month for rent, plus bills, even though I was not earning any commission that first year. Selling to the pharmaceutical industry is not easy, as it can be tough to convince companies to change suppliers. The costs of socializing and enjoying Dublin life were prohibitive, but I managed the best I could.

Zara and I would walk on the pier every day, make our videos, and enjoy the beautiful coastline. I was thankful to be living in such a beautiful location. I was also grateful to be with the company I had joined. I had formed great relationships with some of my colleagues and had started to feel safe and secure there, which was also what I needed at this time.

Dún Laoghaire was a place of peace and healing for me. Zara and I would walk to Dalkey, grab a coffee and then head to Bulloch, a small fishing harbor where, every morning at six, the local fishermen sell their morning's catch. Zara and I spent hours gazing at the sea, drifting off into another world.

Going Out

I had just turned fifty. I was single, but I was in a better emotional space than ever before. I would never have thought I would be celebrating my fiftieth birthday without a partner. Justin had always said he would take me on an exploration cruise for my fiftieth. But here I was in Dublin, single, and in a happier place, but without any fancy plans.

My friend Wendy kindly arranged a surprise party for me at The Bailey Bar, my favorite haunt in the city. She arranged for all my Dublin friends and my work colleagues to be there. I was so surprised, and extremely grateful to Wendy. She had contacted Nigel, and together they had arranged a super night for me.

Would I ever have imagined that at fifty I would be single, and living in Dublin? Not in a million years. But this was where my journey had taken me, so I chose to embrace it. Shortly before my fiftieth birthday, I made a video for my blog in which I said I was the happiest I had been in quite some time. I said that age is only a number, and we should never think we are too old to do anything. I think it was one of my best videos, as I was really speaking from the heart. To me, authenticity is everything, and I believe my honesty is what has always drawn people to my blog. I shared videos of myself out in the city having fun, acting the eejit in a fun, lighthearted way.

For the first time in my life, I was being myself and not trying to fit into anyone else's world, not denying my religion, and not caring whether people liked me. I was reborn as the butterfly I had always wanted to be. No one could tell me not to show off my cleavage or wear certain clothes, no one could tell me to be quiet, and no one could stop me from going out and staying out as late as I wanted. I was free as a bird, and it felt awesome.

Dublin city was my oyster. I was growing into a new person every day. My followers encouraged me with their engagement, and I felt like they all were traveling with me on my journey. I encountered some trolls and bullies. I think some people, who were jealous of my new life, had formed fake profiles to bring me down and make me feel bad for the life I was living. In the past, this would have bothered me and affected my self-esteem, but I had changed since then. I refused to allow any negativity to ruin my new life and my new happiness. I simply blocked them.

My dad had often said, "Denise, when people try to sabotage your character, it says more about them than it does about you."

This is so true, and it has taken me a long time to understand this. Now I will never allow anyone else to bring me down.

For many years, I had tried to fit in with Steve's family and to be who they wanted me to be, but now I was done with pretending to be something that I am not. I was finally happy just being myself and living my life in the way I wanted. If people didn't like me, that was their problem. Never again would I change myself for anyone else. It was a hard-won lesson, but it is one of the biggest life lessons I had to learn. The next man who comes into my life had better not try to change me. I didn't come this far to be controlled or belittled ever again.

I was grateful to have reached fifty in one piece. Now it was time to start living life to the fullest. I decided it was time to start dating for real. By this time my network had grown considerably, and many men contacted me via Facebook or Instagram and asked me out, but I was reluctant to establish a relationship in this way. I simply didn't feel comfortable with it. I met up in real life with only one man who had approached me via social media, and only after we had chatted for some time. It was time to get on the dating apps.

This is where the fun and craziness began. As many of you will already know, it's a very strange experience. Internet dating is a lot like Netflix, in that you often feel overwhelmed by the variety of choice. Once you figure out what you're looking for, you find yourself talking to so many men who want to chat all the time and shower you with compliments. It can be hard to tell who is being genuine. Then, many of them will suddenly stop talking to you after a day or so. This seems somewhat disrespectful, but I guess they are all talking to so many women. I believe there are more women than men on these apps, and that's why the men get away with blue murder. When you stand up for yourself or call someone out on his behavior, he can simply ghost you and move onto someone else.

I had been talking to a guy I liked for some time. When he had suggested meeting in town on a Saturday afternoon, I thought it sounded perfect. I love having wine and nibbles on a weekend afternoon, and if the company is good, that's even better.

I met him in a wine bar just off South William Street. This part of the city always has a great buzz, as it is packed with shops, bars, and restaurants.

As I walked into the bar, I could see him approaching me. I thought, *He isn't bad looking, but let's see what the craic is like.* I was hoping to meet someone fun and confident who could make me laugh.

This guy struck me as being cocksure. He ordered a charcuterie board and a bottle of red wine. He was all about himself and how wonderful he was at his job. I almost didn't need to speak. He was downing his wine quite quickly, and before too long he had ordered us another bottle.

Jeepers, I thought, *I know I can drink, but he is giving me a run for my money.*

After polishing off the second bottle, he said, "Let's have a third."

"No," I said, "that's enough for me."

He said, "I'm supposed to be playing golf in the morning, but I'll cancel it if you invite me to your place."

I was taken aback. "I have only just met you," I said, "I'm not inviting you to my home."

"Your loss," he said with a shrug. "Have a good life." He stood up, put on his coat, and walked out, leaving me with the bill.

I sat there in shock for a few moments before ringing his number. He had already blocked me. I was extremely annoyed, and I felt awful. As I paid the bill, I wondered whether we had been seen by anyone I knew.

On my way home, I knocked on Susan's door. Susan is my beautiful next-door neighbor, who had come over and introduced herself on my first night in the house. I told her what had just happened, and she was horrified on my behalf. She, too, is single, so we have spent many nights talking about how much the dating scene has changed in the last years and how difficult it is to meet men who will treat you with respect.

I was starting to wonder if this was how it was going to be. Had all the men suddenly turned into creeps? Perhaps the world had been changing the whole time I was with Steve, and I just hadn't noticed. The one thing I was sure of was that I didn't like this new state of affairs.

At that time, I didn't want a big relationship, I only wanted to meet a guy I could have fun with. I didn't want anything heavy, just someone to date. I was enjoying my life in Dublin and there were many things I wanted to achieve, but I enjoy male company and I was missing this part of my life.

A few weeks passed. I brushed myself off and went on another date. Jake was a friend of a friend. Although he seemed to be very charming, he would lay it on a bit thick at times. He constantly fed me lines that I sensed were disingenuous. Still, he was attractive and kind, so I decided to give him the benefit of the doubt.

We went on a few dates. One weekend, he came over to my place and we went for a long walk. We came back to mine and were having some wine and food when Nigel phoned.

"Are you with a guy called Jake?" Nigel asked me.

"Yeah, I am," I replied. "Why do you ask?"

"He is also dating my friend," Nigel said. "He was with her last night and was telling her how much he loved her and all that."

"OK, thanks for telling me," I said.

I came off the phone and confronted Jake. He almost died. He couldn't believe he had been caught out.

"Listen," I said, "I have only just met you and this is our fourth date. I am also dating other people, but I am not telling them I love them. I think you have issues around needing to have your ego massaged."

I didn't see him again after that. He was just another player, and I sure didn't need that in my life.

By this stage, I had formed the impression that the dating scene was seriously different to what I had experienced before Steve.

Will I ever meet a genuine guy? Will I be alone for the rest of my life?

I was starting to worry that the latter would prove true. While I had my own issues around trust, I was willing to give it a go and put myself out there.

I went on many dates with very nice men I did not fancy. Their energy was wrong, or they lacked the drive and charisma that I need in a partner. To me, the chemistry and the connection are everything. If those elements aren't present, I would rather be somewhere else enjoying life with my friends or by myself.

Giving Back

I went to Vegas for a holiday with my mates from Belfast, including my close friend, Beverly. It was great to have some time with them, and it had been a while since I had been able to get away. Ever since the move, I had been spending all my money just on living and surviving in Dublin.

Upon returning home I received an e-mail from Frank Diamond, a gorgeous person I had met through the Dublin Chamber. Frank is a former priest who had spent fifteen years working as a missionary in Tanzania before leaving the priesthood and getting married. There is something special about Frank. I love his energy and his sense of stewardship.

Frank is the founder and COO of All Lives are Precious (ALPS), a community-based mental health initiative that offers support and services on emotional wellbeing, including mental health education, free counselling services, and suicide prevention. In his email, he wrote that he would be taking a group of people to Tanzania for ten days with his organization to raise awareness about suicide prevention and mental health. Each participant would be expected to raise at least €2,000 in advance of the trip.

In Tanzania, fourteen people die by suicide each day. We would be going there to deliver a training program in suicide prevention. Having the opportunity to visit Tanzania and to help real people and live with them, instead of staying in a five-star resort, is exactly the kind of trip I had always wanted to make. I have suffered from depression, and have contemplated suicide on more than one occasion, so this cause is very close to my heart. I responded immediately to say that I wanted to participate. I was so excited.

I started my fundraising campaign by organizing an event at the Bailey Bar, my favorite bar in Dublin. John, the manager, let me hire out the place at a discounted rate, and many people donated gifts for the raffle. Frank gave a talk about our upcoming adventure and explained what kind of work we would be doing there. It was a fun night, but we had raised only €250.

OK, I said to myself, *I just need to keep plugging away, and I will eventually get there.*

I received generous donations from friends, social media followers, and the company where I work.

Kevin Davis, a reader of my blog, donated €500. He told me, "I think you are doing something amazing. It's important to raise awareness about suicide prevention, and I want to help you."

When I told him how much I appreciated his support for the cause, he went on to say, "You have helped me so much over the last year. I admire you. Reading your blog has helped me to see that we can all start again, so I thank you."

I couldn't believe my blog was having a positive impact on people's lives. This encouraged me to do even more to help others. I started to feel that starting this blog was one of the best things I had ever done in my life.

Once I had raised the money, I began getting excited and nervous about the trip. I knew I would not have my creature comforts while I was there, but this was all part of seeing the world from a different perspective and it would help me to experience life as so many other people in the world experience it. In many ways, I have been extremely fortunate in life, and I wanted to give something back. The least I could do was to endure life for ten days without a hairdryer, hot showers, and my cozy bed.

On the morning we set off, I was full of excitement. I was also quite nervous but did my best to conceal it. I met Frank and the rest of the team near the check-in counter, and we boarded the plane. We flew to Addis Ababa and caught a connecting flight to Dar es Salaam, where we spent the night at a hotel.

In the morning, the brother of one of Frank's friends from the priesthood picked us up and drove us to the place where we would board the coach to Moshi, our destination. As we straggled toward the coach in the bright, hot sunshine, we were told that the journey would take eight hours.

This will be hard, but I'll survive, I told myself. *We'll have air-conditioning and Wi-Fi on the coach, so it will all be OK.*

As I stepped onto the coach, I was enveloped by even more intense heat and an overpowering smell of BO.

I thought, *How will I do this?*

Frank said, "Denise, you are doing so well. I know this is so out of your comfort zone." He was so lovely.

I looked around. We appeared to be the only foreigners on the bus. I settled in for the journey and firmly told myself, *Stop behaving like a princess. This is all part of the experience, so enjoy it. Live in the moment.*

A few hours into the journey I started to overheat and needed some air, so we stopped for ten minutes before continuing our journey. I had brought along some sweets, and they helped to keep us going. When we had been driving for four hours, it began to rain heavily. It was coming down in sheets and the roads were starting to flood, so I wondered whether we would make it to our destination.

After being on the road for ten hours, we arrived in Moshi. We were welcomed by Frank's friend and former colleague Father Willie, whose brother had brought us to the coach in Dar es Salaam. What a man. I instantly sensed Father Willie's warmth and strength of character, and I was glad I had made this journey. He kindly let us stay at the parish house, which was a lot more comfortable than a cabin and offered respite from the mozzies.

In those ten days I experienced so much, but my memory of the kids stands out the most and will always stay with me. They blew me away with their happiness and their smiling faces. They had nothing, but they loved life. Visiting the orphanage was extremely upsetting to me. I have never considered myself the maternal type, but I couldn't stop holding these precious children. Whenever I picked up a child, they would cry as soon as I attempted to set them back down. It was heartbreaking. I had brought along some of my clothes to give away to people, and it was great to see how happy this made them. It made me feel so warm inside.

During the daytime we would go out and visit various schools, colleges, and developments. In the evenings, we would return to the parish house and have dinner with Father Willie. On several occasions we were joined by other individuals or groups also staying at the parish.

On one evening, a lovely gentleman from the Netherlands joined us for dinner. He took a shine to me, which was flattering, as he was handsome and highly educated. The rest of my group spent much of the following day winding me up about it—all in good fun, of course.

Every day, I posted on my blog about my experiences. My friends and my followers enjoyed reading these updates, particularly as many of them had contributed to our mission. I counted myself very lucky to have been able to go on this trip.

When I came back, I felt like a different person. I realized how important it is to stop and look around sometimes to see how I might be able to benefit the greater good. Sometimes we can be so concerned with material gains and pursuing our idea of success that we forget to give back.

Shortly after I returned home, I was contacted by Lámh Fáilte, a Dublin-based charity that provides outreach and help for the many homeless people in Dublin. Every Saturday night, they run a stall supplying food, clothes, bedding, and hot meals and drinks to homeless people.

I started to do fundraising and to help with preparing the food and running the stall on Saturday evenings. Many of my followers pitched in by volunteering or donating. On my blog I often shared posts about our activities.

I might never have become involved with this initiative if I hadn't made that trip to Tanzania. Visiting Tanzania was a lifechanging experience that helped me to appreciate everything that I have and made me wish I could do more to help. The people of Tanzania, and the happiness and love they showed me, will remain etched on my mind forever.

In Tanzania with ALPS - November 2019

Déjà Vu

Christmas was approaching, and I was on my own yet again. After having been on quite a few disastrous dates, I had started to feel that dating was hard work. My friend Richard and I were chatting on the phone about how hard this time of year is for single people.

Richard is originally from the UK, and for the last twenty-five years he has lived in New York City, where he works in banking. A few years ago, he had moved to Ireland to work for one of the large banks. We had dated for a month and then remained friends, and that is how I had discovered Dún Laoghaire. Richard had eventually moved back to NYC because he missed his kids, who still live there, but we have always stayed in touch.

Richard said, "Why don't you come over here and be single with me?"

"OK," I said, "You are on."

I booked my ticket straight away.

I had my mum over for Christmas dinner, so she wouldn't be alone. On Boxing Day, I flew to NYC and spent a fabulous six days with Richard. We rang in the year 2020 in style. As he knows the city inside out, I was able to experience New York in a way that most tourists don't. Richard was dating but had not yet met the right person. We compared notes on the dating scenes in Dublin and NYC, and our experiences weren't that different. It seemed it was just as difficult for men as for women.

I think the world has changed with the creation of dating apps. They provide a playground where narcissists and people with all kinds of underlying issues can prey on vulnerable and lonely individuals. I can honestly say I hate the apps. I never dreamed that I would be in this position after having men chase me all my life. There was never any shortage of men asking me out.

It can be hard to value yourself highly when you are constantly being judged according to superficial and arbitrary standards. You must prove your worth through a few profile photos and perhaps a couple of text messages. If you don't say the right thing or have the right look, people swipe left and move to the next thing. After a while, it starts to dig away at your self-esteem and make you feel unworthy of love.

I flew home from NYC on my birthday. Spending time with Richard had made me realize how much I missed being in a relationship. I decided to try Bumble, an app on which women take the lead. Men can choose you only if you choose them first. I had heard that on Bumble there were fewer players who are just looking to hook up and more people who are seeking real relationships.

Soon after joining Bumble, I matched with a cute guy called Stewart. He was originally from Dublin and was back home visiting, but he lived in Spain. We went out for dinner, and he seemed nice, exciting, and fun. He was blond, and not too tall but kept himself very fit. Meeting him restored my belief that there might still be some good guys out there. He came on quite strong and would text me non-stop. I quite enjoyed this, as it had been six years since I had been in a relationship.

We met up for another date. We had great chemistry and a real connection. He invited me out to meet his friends. Leinster were playing, so we would watch the rugby and go to lunch. To me, this was such a fab date, as I love rugby and meeting new people. I was excited to meet his friends. I took an instant liking to his friend Ann, a lovely bright, bubbly woman. She was happily married, but she had also undergone a difficult time in the dating world before meeting her husband, so we had lots in common.

I was thrilled to have met Stewart. He was the first man I had really fancied since my breakup with Steve. We went out a few more times, and he extended his stay in Ireland. He was in no hurry to get back, as he was already retired at the age of fifty-one. Being a very driven person, he had made enough money to stop working earlier than most people do. While I admired that about him, I also noticed he was quite big-headed about his achievements. He seemed to constantly seek praise from others.

No one is perfect, I told myself, *not even you. Give him a chance.*

Stewart would go for a cycle or a run and then send me his performance stats. I found this slightly off-putting, but I went along with it.

In the back of my mind, I wondered, *Is this guy all about himself?*

Not long after we had started dating, Stewart invited me to go to Portugal for the weekend with him and his gang of friends.

Ann said, "Please come, Denise! It will be great fun."

I said, "Yeah, why not?"

We had a fabulous holiday. I was feeling great about everything. I was happy in my life, and things seemed to be getting better all the time. I felt at home in Dublin and had been meeting lots of people, I was developing in my career and earning more money, and I was excited about my new relationship.

I had noticed that after spending extended periods of time with me, Stewart would pull away from me. When we returned from our holiday, he totally withdrew for quite some time. Everything I had learned from Clare came to the forefront.

I asked myself, *Is he emotionally available? Am I heading down the same road again? Is he a narcissist? Is he focused only upon himself?*

It was all too familiar: a man with high energy, who seemed averse to forming a real relationship, had me wanting to change him and make him connect with me at a deeper level.

Apocalypse

By February, Stewart was dividing his time between his home in Spain and my place in Dublin. When he was around, I would devote a lot of time to him, so I kept a full social calendar whenever he was away. I was always busy catching up with my friends or attending networking events, and I sometimes felt it bothered him that I wasn't in constant contact with him.

A woman called Natalie contacted me through my blog and invited me to a big charity event in Dublin. I invited my friend Wendy along, and we got all dressed up. The event would be at House, a trendy bar and restaurant on Leeson Street that was one of my favorite Saturday night haunts. I loved the atmosphere, and the music was always awesome. You could not get me off the dancefloor. If anyone needed to find me, it would have been there or at The Bailey, on Duke Street, where I had hosted my fundraising event for ALPS. John, the manager, always looked after me. I just loved going there to people-watch.

Wendy and I headed off to meet Natalie. She turned out to be a blond bombshell, and a breath of fresh air. She was gorgeous and fun, exactly the type of person to whom I could relate. We were like sisters, as we looked similar and had the same mad, fun energy. Natalie became an extremely great friend after that first night, and I am so glad I met her.

Throughout the entire evening, Stewart kept texting and phoning me. This raised a red flag, as I guessed he was feeling insecure and wondering what I was doing. At the same time, I found it reassuring. I slipped into my old pattern, of not realizing I was being love bombed, and simply succumbing to the dopamine rush instead. I felt that this obsessive behavior meant that he must really like me, and it made me feel more secure in the relationship. After having discussed this so many times with Clare, I should have been able to recognize this behavior. I guess I always need to learn things the hard way.

My mind was telling me Stewart might not be the right man for me, but my heart kept telling me how much I liked him. The heart won, and I decided to keep things going. I loved waking up to his morning texts and receiving his many calls over the course of the day. Steve had been the type of guy to be in constant contact, and I had missed this. I felt loved and wanted again.

Stewart invited me to meet him and his friends in Paris to attend the Six Nations Rugby Tournament 2020. The tournament had commenced on February 1 and was scheduled to run through to March 14. We made all the arrangements and were due to head off in March to watch Ireland play France in Round Five. I was thrilled. I loved spending time with Steve and his friends, and I knew we would have a great time.

For some time, we had been hearing about the coronavirus outbreak in Asia and North America. In late January, it had spread to Europe, with the first confirmed cases appearing in Bordeaux and Paris. By the end of February, the first case of coronavirus in Ireland was confirmed by the Department of Health.

In early March, it was announced that the last four games of the tournament—including the match we had planned to attend—would be postponed. We briefly considered meeting in Paris regardless, but France was preparing to implement a nationwide lockdown, so we canceled our trip.

Stewart and I were gutted that we wouldn't be seeing each other. St. Patrick's Day was coming up, and it would be a bank holiday weekend. Stewart suggested that I visit him in Spain. I could fly out on the Friday and return on the Wednesday—the day after St. Patrick's.

I said, "Yeah, why not? I am sure it will be OK."

I booked my flight.

On March 11, two days before I was due to fly to Spain, the World Health Organization officially declared COVID-19 a pandemic. That same day, Ireland reported its first coronavirus death. The very next day, Ireland instated its first restrictions and social distancing measures against COVID-19, which included the closure of schools, colleges, and childcare facilities, and bans on indoor gatherings of more than a hundred people. Where possible, everyone was working from home, though shops, bars, and restaurants were still open.

I left on the Friday as planned. On the flight to Spain, I was surrounded by empty seats. I wondered whether I had done the right thing. It was too late—we had already taken off. I had a few gin and tonics to ease my nerves.

After we landed, I was delighted to see Stewart waiting at the arrivals area. We went to the beach and had lunch. He seemed to be extremely anxious about the pandemic. Although I was still somewhat relaxed about it, this was during the first wave when there was still a high likelihood of dying from it, so his reaction seemed perfectly reasonable. I didn't think too much of it. It was just so great to see him and be able to spend time with him.

During my stay, I learned a bit more about Stewart. I observed some behavior that alarmed me. He displayed several obsessive-compulsive tendencies that led me to wonder whether he has OCD. When he was at my place, he had always seemed quite relaxed.

I could not tell whether this behavior had been triggered by his considerable anxiety about the pandemic. Perhaps he had always been this way, and I was noticing it only now because we were spending time together on his territory for the first time. It may have been a combination of both factors.

We can spend time with a person and believe that we know them, but it can take a very long time before we see who they really are. All too often I have let myself get so swept up in the excitement of meeting someone new and connecting with them, that I completely overlook their unhealthy or harmful character traits, even when they are staring me right in the face. Over time, I have learned to stay calm, and take the time to go deeper, to try to see the person as they really are. At fifty-one, I have a better understanding of people, and I am learning to follow my instincts. It has taken me many years and many mistakes to get where I am today. As they say, better late than never.

During my time in Spain, the news continued to escalate. The day after I arrived, Ireland was added to the US travel ban list. There were rumors that the EU would also instate a travel ban, so I decided to fly home a day early.

After I arrived home on St. Patrick's Day, Taoiseach Leo Varadkar announced further measures to contain the spread of COVID-19, including the closure of pubs and bars. He asked everyone to start 'cocooning' by restricting the number of people with whom they come into contact and practicing social distancing.

On the same day, the EU implemented a thirty-day ban on all non-essential travel between its member states. (This would later be extended until May 15, and then extended until June 15.)

The following day, much of Europe went into lockdown. I counted myself fortunate to have managed to get away one last time. Although my trip had been somewhat marred by all the stress and fear surrounding the pandemic, it had been lovely to spend some time with Stewart. I had no idea of when I might be able to see him again.

On March 27, Ireland was placed on full lockdown. You were allowed to leave your home only for the purposes of exercise or grocery shopping, and you had to remain within a two-kilometer radius of your home. Like many others, I was terrified of spending the next two weeks cooped up at home in complete solitude.

I went for a walk with my neighbor Susan. We both live alone and were wondering how we would cope with a two-week lockdown. We advised each other to make plenty of cocktails and to try to make the best of it until things returned to normal.

As the company for whom I work supplies to the pharmaceutical industry, I was issued a document that permitted me to keep traveling around Ireland for work. I offered to deliver our labels, as I was eager to get out of the house. I was travelling to Galway, Cork, Limerick, and anywhere else I was asked to go. It was very hot, and I would often pop to the beach before heading back.

Thanks to this permit, I was also able to keep visiting my mother, who was suffering with dementia but still lived at home. I am grateful for this, as I know many people were not able to see their loved ones for a very long time.

I was much better off than many other people, but it was still very lonely and frightening. I started making and sharing fun videos of my travels to cheer up my friends and my followers. I discovered TikTok, which was a godsend. It allowed me to express myself by having fun and hamming it up. In the evenings, Stewart would video call me, and we would chat and drink wine.

On April 10, Taoiseach Varadkar came on the television again to announce that lockdown was extended for a further three weeks, until May 5. Before our eyes, the world was changing in ways we could never have imagined. I wondered how long the current situation would continue. I wasn't seeing any of my friends, and I was feeling lonely.

I felt alone for the first time since moving to Dublin, and it was the strangest feeling ever. If it hadn't been for Susan, Zara, my blog, and my work, I am not sure how I would have managed. At times like these, it's important to count one's blessings. I was grateful that the pier was right on my doorstep and that the weather was great. Susan and I could walk to the pier or share a bottle of wine and listen to music together.

On May 5, the restrictions were eased ever so slightly, and we were permitted to travel up to five kilometers from our homes to exercise. As the EU travel ban was still in place and would remain so for the foreseeable future, there was no knowing when I would be able to meet Stewart again. I had begun to wonder whether there was any point in continuing our relationship. Just as I was thinking this over, Stewart texted me to express the same sentiment.

Things between us ended amicably. I felt it had been good while it lasted, and I was not certain we would have been compatible going forward. *Perhaps this is just my luck,* I thought. I was beginning to wonder if I would ever find a love that would endure. It always seemed to end for one reason or another.

After Stewart and I had broken up, I felt even more isolated in lockdown. It had been a source of great comfort to have that special someone, with whom I could check in over the course of the day and video chat in the evenings. I stayed in regular phone contact with my friends, including a few new friends I had met through my blog.

Whenever the restrictions were eased for a while and we could travel a little further afield, we would meet up in person. I often went to my friend Natalie's house. Sometimes we would meet in the park for drinks, or she would come here to the pier. We tried to make the best out of a bad situation, but it was tough.

The blog helped keep me going. I knew that my followers might be going through all kinds of horrible things at this time, and I didn't want to bring them down with my issues and insecurities. I tried to put on a brave and happy face. This was a good thing, as it provided my life with some structure and brightened my mood on the days I didn't want to get out of bed.

Life during the pandemic affected each of us in different ways. For many of us, it completely changed our lives. I felt that the life I had created was over, and I wondered what really lay ahead for me.

Reopening

In July, restaurants were allowed to open, if the tables were spaced a certain distance apart. Restaurant clientele would be required to wear masks when they were not seated, and servers would have to always wear them. Susan and I made a reservation at one of our favorite local spots—the award-winning restaurant at The Haddington House Hotel, which was right around the corner from us.

We had a beautiful evening and were so excited that life might be returning to normal. I was so happy to be out. A reporter from the Irish Times came up to us and asked us to talk about how we were feeling. A photo of the two of us, sitting in the restaurant enjoying some light freedom, appeared in the paper the next day alongside our comments.

As single people living alone, we had both found the isolation of lockdown very difficult to bear. While couples who lived together during lockdown were lucky to have had each other, I am sure it wasn't easy spending all hours of the day cooped up together without any distractions or outlets. We all have suffered in some way.

During this time, I drifted apart from some of my friends, due to differences of opinion on various matters surrounding the pandemic. Like many people, I took the proper precautions while still trying to live my life. When I saw other people judging or even publicly chastising their friends for the choices they were making, it made me feel so anxious. I felt that the government, my friends, and even total strangers were trying to control me.

I needed human contact and simply could not sit at home alone for twenty-four hours a day, seven days a week. Throughout the rolling lockdowns, I would occasionally get on the apps to connect with men. I would meet guys outdoors for coffee or a walk, but it was not always worthwhile. Most of them were uptight and nervous on these dates.

One day, my friend Natalie said, "Why don't we organize a night out and make the best of a bad situation?"

I said, "Yes, that sounds perfect."

My friend Beverley came down from Belfast, which was against the rules, but at this stage we didn't care. A group of six of us decided to stay at a hotel in town and go to the Bailey, which was serving food and drinks outside. We figured we could go there until they closed at eight, and then have a gathering in the hotel and create our own fun. The Bailey reserved a large suite for us at the nearby Fitzwilliam Hotel, which also belongs to them.

We were like kids going to a school disco for the first time. It felt so good to be able to get dressed up and go out again after all this time. It was almost too good to be true. We had a great night at the Bailey and then returned to the hotel, where we danced the night away in our hotel suite. The next day, we all headed home, feeling that we had really needed that release.

About a week later, John, the manager of the Bailey, and I both received a letter from the Advertising Authority of Ireland. The letter stated that I had received free services from the Bailey and had posted about them on my social media without stating that they had been given to me free of charge.

I knew that when you receive anything for free and post it on your social media, you are supposed to mention in the post that it is a paid advertisement; however, the Bailey has never given me anything for free. John simply looked after us well, and I always posted about being there. I had done nothing wrong.

To this day, I have my suspicions about who it was that lodged this complaint. The fact that someone was going to such lengths to make false accusations against me made me feel like I was back at school. We were living through a pandemic, and all this person could think of was how to hurt me.

A week later, my boss received a letter that said I had been making videos while I was supposed to be working. Fortunately, my boss already knew all about my blog. He simply said, "Someone is very jealous of you."

He told me he thought it was shocking that someone was attempting to get me the sack.

I was so upset. I made a video in which I talked about what had happened and posted it on my blog. In hindsight, I probably should not have given this individual the satisfaction of seeing how hurt I was. I had often been the target of other people's jealousy, but I thought this would not happen once I reached a certain age. How wrong I was.

Christmas came and went. The pandemic was still ongoing, but we were allowed to travel with a PCR test. My friend Brenda suggested spending the New Year break in Lanzarote, where the case incidence was relatively low.

"Yes," I said. "Let's do it."

I was eager to get away, as I had heard that the government was considering implementing another full lockdown in January. I thought, *I can't keep doing this. How will I get through another major lockdown?*

Brenda and I headed off to Lanzarote for five days. The plane was packed. I hadn't told anyone I was going, as I didn't want to deal with people judging me. I had met Brenda through my blog. She had been though a very difficult time with her husband and was still struggling, so we both needed a break.

It was pretty quiet in Lanzarote, so all we did was lie on the beach, but it was heaven to be able to go to a bar and have a drink. We met a few guys from Dublin who were there for the same reason, and we hung out with them in the evenings. It was so good to get away.

We returned home feeling refreshed and were slightly better equipped to face the news that Ireland was going back into lockdown. Many people were scared to leave their homes and I understand why, but I was never scared of getting the virus. I believed that if I did contract it and ended up dying of it, then that was my destiny. I was going to live the best I could.

I felt as if my life was disappearing right in front of my eyes. We had undergone a full year of rolling lockdowns, and there was still no end in sight. I had just passed my fifty-second birthday. Would this be my life forever? I began to feel very down and anxious, even though I knew I was much better off than many other people. I had just been on vacation, my job enabled me to get out and about, and I was living in the perfect area, but my own deep sadness was coming out. I was looking back on my life and wondering what I had achieved. I questioned how and why I had come to be on my own at this age.

I had also noticed I was feeling out of touch with my sexuality and my femininity. It had been a year since I had been with anyone. Stewart and I had shared great chemistry, and I missed that. In the meantime, I had been propositioned by many men, but I wasn't attracted to any of them. I can't have sex with a man unless I fancy them. I would rather be alone.

I am a tactile person who loves physical affection, and I was starting to really crave it. I was close with a few men, but only as friends. I missed hugs, kisses, and intimacy. We all need it—I know I do. I needed that skin-on-skin feeling. I didn't want to go through the next lockdown alone. I decided to give Tinder another shot.

I thought, *What's the worst that can happen? I might end up talking to yet another emotionally unavailable man, or a married man, or a player, or a normal, boring person. What else would I be doing with my time? Watching Netflix and drinking wine!*

I joined up again, and it was the same as ever. Many of the men on dating apps seem to want a pen pal, and I simply don't have the time or the energy to write a thousand text messages before meeting someone face to face—or perhaps never meeting them. I want to move things forward and to find out if the person is worth my time.

Within the first few days, I matched with a lot of guys. As I have mentioned, I am like a witch. From reading a few texts, I can usually identify a guy's personality type. If I sense they are not on my wavelength, I will move on quite quickly.

On Day Two, I matched with a guy called Sean, who seemed interesting but was not particularly good-looking. Looks are not a big thing for me; it is all about the connection, and I usually need to meet a person to gauge that. After we had exchanged two messages, he asked me to give him my number so he could call me.

I was caught off-guard by this, but at the same time, I liked that he was being so direct. Giving out my number was no big deal, as I could always block him if I needed to. Many people are afraid to move too quickly on the apps. I don't get that, as I think you can get to know a person more quickly when you speak to them on the phone.

When he phoned, I was in bed cuddling Zara. I instantly liked his voice. He was fun to talk to, and he loved a laugh. I liked that he seemed to be a very driven person who pursued his dreams and would not let anything get in his way. We ended up talking for two hours. Before ending our chat, he asked me where I would be the following day.

"Galway," I said.

"On the way back, would you fancy meeting for a coffee in Dún Laoghaire?" he asked me.

"Yeah, I would."

I remember feeling happy as I was driving to Galway. I knew I would like this man when I met him. He seemed exciting, and I loved the way he didn't mess around and didn't waste any time. *A little like Justin*, I thought.

We met outside a coffee shop. It was early January, and it was cold but sunny. I had been on so many dates by this point in my life that meeting for the first time was cool for me. I never felt nervous. I was always just myself, and if they didn't like me, that was fine. I wasn't going to start trying to be someone else.

As we walked towards each other, I saw that he was wearing a hat and a pair of really baggy joggers. I thought he hadn't made much of an effort. He had looked better in his photos than he did in real life. He asked me what I would like to drink, and I said a coffee would be great. He said I could wait there while he popped inside to get our drinks.

As I waited for him to come back, I remember thinking he wasn't at all what I had expected, but at least he seemed friendly. I thought, *Well, it's only for coffee.*

We stood in the cold, and I talked about my work and about COVID. At the time, there wasn't that much else going on. He seemed uninterested in the conversation. After we had been chatting for about thirty minutes, he said, "It's really cold. Do you fancy coming to my house for dinner some time? I know this may seem a little forward, but it's not like we can go out for dinner, and we can hardly keep meeting like this in the cold."

I said, "Sure, we can chat later and arrange something."

As I left, I thought, *I am not sure about this man. He seems a bit pushy, but unless I meet him properly, I will never know.*

When I arrived home, he phoned me.

"Do you want to come down tonight? You can bring your dog for safety."

I thought, *Jesus—Zara would lick him to death rather than bite him!*

He said he had not been in contact with anyone. I told him I would think it over and call him back.

Then I phoned Susan and asked her what she thought I should do.

She said, "Go on, sure, why not? Life is so boring, you might as well. Give me his number, text me his address, and keep in touch."

We were not supposed to travel further than five kilometers from home, and Sean lived about seven kilometers away, but I decided to risk it. I phoned him back and told him I would drive down.

When I arrived at his house, he was better dressed and was no longer wearing the hat, but he looked a lot older than he had earlier that day. I suddenly didn't find him attractive. Zara and I went inside. I decided I could always use her as an excuse to leave early.

"I have ordered Indian food," he said. "Is that OK?"

"Yeah, of course. I love Indian food," I replied.

Zara was sniffing every part of the house to make sure she couldn't detect the presence of another dog. I hoped she wouldn't pee on the floor or anything.

Although Sean was quite charismatic, he also seemed to be quite closed off. I reminded myself that he might simply be feeling awkward. I was in a stranger's house on what was practically still our first date, but how else were we going to meet? Everything about this situation was abnormal, and we had to make the best of it. It would be another six months before things opened up again, though we did not know this at the time.

Sean was interesting, and he seemed interested in me. We both had travelled a lot. He was impressed that I had dropped everything and moved to Dublin by myself.

"Fair play," he said. "I couldn't do that, but I respect you for doing it."

After we had been there for a few hours, Zara and I headed off home.

The next day I told Susan all about it. We would always share our dating stories with each other. We called ourselves the Basement Girls, and we thought our chat sessions would have made a great TV show.

Susan said, "That sounds like a nice evening. Sure, just see how it goes and when you hear from him again."

"I'm not sure about him," I said, "but maybe he'll grow on me. It's early days, as I didn't know him at all."

A few days later, he texted me to say he was coming to Dún Laoghaire for a bike ride, and did I fancy meeting?

I said, "Yeah, that would be nice."

When we met, I still thought he was not that good-looking. He had sharp features and was losing his hair. I thought, *I will not worry about that. Let's just keep meeting. No harm in that.* I was bored, and this was a welcome distraction.

Two days later, we met for a walk along Sandymount Strand. Although the weather was not warm, it was sunny, so it was very pleasant. I found him very interesting and enjoyed all his stories about his life.

I felt he was very like Justin. He had the same drive, and his attitude to life was similar. He didn't appear to care what anyone thought of him, and I liked that. He told me he had previously been married for over twenty-five years and had remained faithful to his wife throughout their marriage. This was one of the things I liked most about him, especially as I still had issues around trust.

He may have been lying for all I know, but at this stage I wanted to believe him. I had already begun to feel that he talked too much about how successful he was and would often brag about his achievements. Most of the time, he would do all the talking and I would listen. It was interesting, nonetheless.

It was Thursday, and he invited me and Zara to come down on the Saturday. He said we could go for a walk, and he would cook dinner. We could stay in the spare room if we wanted. I thought this would be nice, as I enjoyed his company and was intrigued by him for some reason. I wanted to get to know him better, so I accepted his invitation. I said to Zara as I packed our bags, "We are spending a night away from home, so you had better behave yourself."

She started squealing, as she does when I put on her lead and guide her to the car. She gets so excited, almost to the point of hysterics, at the idea of getting out.

On Saturday, Zara and I made the journey to Sean's place. We all went for a long walk, and he prepared oysters and steak for dinner. I was thrilled. After all this time, it felt good to have a guy doing lovely things for me. I noticed that Sean was very exact about everything in his house, including how to sort the recycling and how to load the dishwasher. It made me feel a little awkward at times.

We spent a cozy evening just watching TV. It was so nice. I realized how much I had been missing male company. This time, I found him more attractive, but he wasn't very warm. He seemed quite closed.

We spent the night. Zara slept in the lounge, in her own bed. She didn't make a fuss about this, which surprised me, as she always liked to be close to me. I had decided to sleep in his bed, as I missed getting hugs and kisses. However, I never received any cuddles that night. He was pretty cold, which was fine.

The next morning, he started to initiate sex. I had never had a one-night stand, but I but I said to myself, *Feck it, I am a fifty-one-year-old woman, and I can do as I please.* I had sex with him, as I felt I needed the intimacy, and I thought we would be spending time together.

It was the strangest experience of my life. He never kissed me, as he said he didn't like kissing, and the sex made me feel as if I was a rubber blow-up doll. I didn't enjoy it and slightly regretted having gone along with it. Afterwards, he asked us to go to the park with him instead of leaving straight away.

I said, 'OK, we can do that."

We went for a walk, and then I said, "We are going to head home now."

As I left, I remember thinking he might have some intimacy issues, as I was almost like a doll to him. Then I thought that perhaps he simply hadn't felt that connected to me and it might improve, so I decided not to dwell on it. Sometimes having sex with someone for the first time can be awkward. We didn't know each other, after all. I thought that I liked him and would like to get to know him better, but that it would probably take a while to get to know him.

A week passed, and I had heard nothing from him. I was feeling pretty flat about it. I messaged him via Whatsapp just to say I hoped that all was well, and to let me know if he fancied a walk. I could see that he was online but had not opened my message. All he had to do was say, "Hi, I am busy, I have a lot going on and I will get back to you."

I was upset to think he had ghosted me. We had spent some time getting to know each other, so to be cast aside without any warning or explanation made me feel used. It brought back the pain of Steve's rejection of me and triggered my old insecurities. As the days went on, my pain turned to anger. My friends all agreed he was not a well-mannered man.

I was beginning to think that this dating game was not for me. Maybe it was easier to be alone. At least I wouldn't have to deal with all this nonsense. We were living in a pandemic, so I couldn't even go out and have fun to recover from how I felt. All I could do was stay home, drink wine and feel sorry for myself. The longer his silence continued, the more annoyed I became.

After about nine days, Sean texted me. I ignored it.

He phoned me a few hours later, and I wasn't sure whether to answer. Finally, I picked up.

"What do you want?" I demanded.

"What's wrong?" he said.

"I messaged you over a week ago, and you did not even have the manners to reply," I said. "In my world, if I spend the weekend with someone, I expect them to communicate with me, even if it is just to say you are busy and will get back to me."

He said he had been busy, and that he had split with someone only a few months before and was not sure about getting into another relationship so soon."

I said, "Was I asking you for anything?"

"No, I suppose not," he replied.

"Well, then you clearly don't possess any manners," I said. "All you had to do was tell me."

He said, "I'm sorry. Can we meet for a coffee in a few days?"

I said I would think about it. Looking back on it now, I wonder if he had tried to patch things up with his ex in the meantime, and it hadn't worked out. Who knows? Whatever the reason, going AWOL for nine days is a red flag. I should not have given him another chance, but I did.

I think this is where my triggers were activated. During his absence, I believed had failed to earn his love and desire. Instead of being scared off, I wanted even more to win him over. Whether or not this was a conscious and tactical strategy on his part, from that day onwards, he love bombed me and I became totally hooked on him.

During the first few months of our relationship, we couldn't really go out and do things, as we were still in lockdown. We just walked, cycled, and cooked. I fancied him a lot. Even though he was not a particularly handsome man, he had a certain charm, and I loved his energy. He was very much like me in that he was impatient and driven.

I introduced him to my friends in Dublin, and he invited them to his house for drinks one evening. They all felt he was fun and that we were well matched. I was beginning to think I was lucky to have met him.

On St. Patrick's Day, we went to the pier to get takeout and drink wine outside. I loved spending time with Sean and my friends. We always made the best of things. It didn't feel so bad being in lockdown when you had someone to share it with.

One day, Natalie suggested, "Why don't we have a small party at Sean's house?"

I said, "Yeah, okay. I will ask him."

Sean thought it was a great idea, so Felim, Natalie, and I went over to his place and we all had food and drinks and danced into the small hours. I loved that Sean could get along so well with my friends and that he knew how to have a good time. I need to be with someone who is spontaneous, up for a laugh, and a go-getter. I believed he had all these qualities.

Once I had become very attached to Sean and was spending most weekends at his house, he made it clear that Zara was no longer welcome there. He didn't like her, and she had soiled his rug. I told him that accidents happen, and we would make sure it didn't happen again. I begged him to allow her to just sleep in her bed on the floor, but he refused. One weekend, he allowed her to come along if she stayed in the bathroom. She whimpered so much, and I couldn't bear it. I couldn't allow my baby to suffer, so I said that will not happen again.

Zara was so attached to me that she would cry all night if she wasn't with me. I would sometimes leave her with Susan or with my dog minder, but I was never happy doing so. The solution would have been to have Sean stay over at my apartment more often, but he said he didn't like it. I could see what was happening here. He was trying to control me by making me choose between him and Zara. I liked him and I loved Zara, so I was caught in a quandary. I tried my best to make it work without neglecting Zara.

In the short time I knew him, we had many arguments about this and other issues. He was very aggressive with me when I made the smallest mistake in his house or while driving. When I told him he was blowing things out of proportion, he would always come back with a manipulative story around it, and I would start to question my own thoughts. He made it sound like I was the one who was overreacting, and I would almost believe it. He would never agree to do anything I wanted to do. We always did what he wanted. When we ordered food, he would always select the restaurant, as he said he knew better than me.

Deep down, I knew that I was accepting a type of behavior that I would not normally stand for. Many of my past loves had manipulated me, but no one had ever simply overpowered me. I had never experienced this bullying type of behavior before, and because I was lonely and had grown attached to him, I found it hard just to walk away.

One morning in April, I was getting ready to go to work when I heard someone banging on my front door.

It was Susan. "Get out!" she screamed. "The building is on fire!"

I was shocked. I ran outside and saw that the roof was on fire.

Oh God, I thought. *What will I do? I love my apartment. I don't want to have to move.*

The fire brigade arrived and were able to extinguish the fire. Some of the water had dripped into my apartment, but fortunately it had not caused that much damage. The upper floors had been ruined, and those tenants had to move out.

I rang Sean and told him what had happened.

He said, "OK, I am on my way down."

When he arrived, he said, "What a mess! You will need to find a new place to live."

I was used to him being very pragmatic, but I was surprised by his complete lack of empathy in this moment.

"I am so upset," I said. "This is my home and I love living here."

He said, "It's a dump. Just move on and get another place."

"Don't you understand how I feel?" I asked him.

"No," he said. "Listen, you needed someone here, and I came. I don't do hugs and affection and telling you everything will be OK. You just have to deal with it. I'm showing you I care by being here now."

I thought, *I need a hug. I need someone who would tell me everything's going to be OK, instead of telling me my needs are irrelevant or inappropriate.*

After the fire brigade had left, things calmed down. I had been told I would be allowed to stay in my place, at least until they sent back a fire cert, which would take a few weeks. That night, I told Susan about how Sean had flat-out refused to give me the kind of support I had told him I needed. She said she felt he was emotionally detached, as he had not expressed any empathy or emotion towards either of us despite what we had been through that day.

A few weeks later, Susan and I were told we would have to leave our apartments after all. I felt scared and anxious. I had lived in this apartment for three years, ever since moving to Dublin, and it was all I knew. Where would I go now? What would I do? I loved living in Dún Laoghaire and didn't want to leave the area.

I tearfully rang Sean, who said, "It's no big deal, I will help you look for a place."

"It is a big deal to me," I replied. "You just don't understand."

"I just don't get attached to property," he said smugly.

Considering how protective of his house he was, I doubted that very much.

"Well, that's you, and not me," I said. "And I don't really want to have to move in the middle of a pandemic."

Nothing lasts forever in my world, and I should have been used to it by now. I had to start searching for a new place. I told myself that maybe it was time for me to find a bigger house anyway. Finding a new place to live was much harder than I had ever imagined. Rents had skyrocketed, and almost all the apartments I saw didn't allow pets.

I was really starting to panic. I thought I might have to go back to the North, which I didn't want to do. I was happy visiting, and it will always be my home, but I didn't want to move back. My life was now in Dublin, and I didn't want to leave Sean.

Meanwhile, Susan had found a fabulous house with a garden. It was just up the hill from us. She said, "Why don't we take it between us?"

I thought this was a grand idea. Susan had become a close friend, and Zara loved her, so it was the perfect solution.

It was June, and lockdown had ended. Restaurants had reopened, and I was excited that I could finally go out on a proper date with Sean. I told him I wanted to go to the Bailey. It had been so long, and I had missed it. I also wanted to go to Browne Thomas, a beautiful department store on Grafton Street. I had not been out shopping in six months, so I was looking forward to it with great anticipation.

The sun was shining when I arrived at Sean's house, eager to embark upon our outing. He said he had changed his mind. He didn't fancy it.

"What?" I couldn't believe what I was hearing. "I have been wanting to do this for six months, so if you don't want to come, I will go by myself. I am fed up with sitting at home."

"OK, OK. I'll go," he said.

We headed out, but his sudden change of heart had already flattened my spirits. I had been so excited about spending a lovely, fun, happy day in the city for the first time with him, and he couldn't have cared any less.

We went into the Bailey, and John, the manager, was so happy to see me. He gave us a great table outside, and we ordered a bottle of rosé.

I said to Sean, "I am so happy to be here."

As always, he had to shoot me down. "It's just OK," he said.

He ogled the woman who was sitting beside me.

"She has some body on her," he said.

I was a little taken back by this, but I wasn't going to take the bait. I sensed that he was saying it mainly to provoke a reaction. He resented me for dragging him out against his will, so he didn't want me to have a good time and was trying to make me feel bad. I wouldn't give him the satisfaction.

"Yeah, she is gorgeous," I said, "and so is her partner. Just look at him."

He promptly changed the subject.

This was our first outing, and already he was trying to put me down.

About an hour later, these two guys I knew happened to come walking by. They came over and joined us for the rest of the afternoon. Then we all moved to Kehoes Pub, which was right around the corner. We sat outside, as there were still restrictions in place, and no-one could go inside.

Each of the guys took me aside and said, "Denise, you are too good for that man. He's rude, and we don't like the way he speaks to you."

"He seems like an angry guy. You could do a lot better."

I wasn't alarmed by this, as a few of my friends had been saying similar things to me.

On the way home, I brought it up, and Sean started shouting at me. He kept saying that I was the one who was being stupid. He was fine.

"I don't want this anymore, Sean," I said. "I value myself too much. I will not tolerate you trying to undermine me and put me down."

He said he was sorry, and that he wanted us to go to bed and start over the next day. I went along with it. In my heart of hearts, I knew he was being emotionally abusive, and that it was slowly getting worse.

One of my friends had been telling me, "Sean is a narcissist. You need to get out of this relationship."

At that time, I didn't fully understand the meaning of the word *narcissist*, so I felt she was overreacting. I stayed with him because I really wanted to make the relationship work. I still believed I could fix him.

We were nearing the end of June. Susan and I were due to move into the new house on the first of July.

When I asked Sean to help me with the move, he said, "No, I don't help with things like that. Anyway, I will be playing golf. I bought you a bottle of perfume. That's my way of saying *good luck in the new house*."

I was so hurt.

On moving day, my work let me use the work van. My colleague drove it and helped us with the move.

All my friends were asking me, "Where is Sean?"

I was so embarrassed, particularly as they had all gone out of their way to be there.

"He isn't coming," I finally admitted.

My friends were horrified. They said I needed to wise up and get rid of him. I knew they were right, but I couldn't break away.

I kept seeing Sean. Over time, his behavior grew increasingly erratic. I felt like I was dating Dr. Jekyll and Mr. Hyde. When I arrived at his house, I was never sure which one I was going to meet. On some days he would be so lovely, and we would have a wonderful time together. He would show me love and tell me he loved me. On other days, he completely withdrew from me.

Sean had a mad temper. He would blow up at me over the smallest of things. He would tear me to pieces and make me feel worthless. He wanted to be praised all the time, but he rarely paid me a compliment. He said he shouldn't have to do that, but we all need our partners to make us feel special. This was the first time I had been with a man who did not appreciate me.

Sean was the first person I had loved since Steve, and this was the first serious relationship I'd had in eight years. I was very sexually attracted to him, but he was unable to give me the affection and TLC to which I was accustomed. He demanded affection but was not willing to give affection. He wanted me to rub his back, but he would never do it to me.

There were days when I looked at myself and thought, *What is happening to you? What are you becoming?*

I came to understand why it is so hard for abused women to leave their abusers. The trauma bonds you to your torturer, and since you can't leave them, all you can do is try to change into what they want. You just keep changing, like a chameleon.

When he was good, he was great, but his constant putdowns and his refusal to show me love was starting to affect my personality. When we walked along the street, he would often walk ahead of me.

I would say, "Can you take my hand?"

He would say, "Why? Come on, you don't need my hand."

I was trying to survive on the tiny crumbs of love he showed me, and I could see how damaging this was becoming for me.

In July, I brought him up home to the North to meet my friends. We had a super time and they liked him, but they also said, "We are not sure why he is still so distant with you, when you have been together for seven months."

I was very up and down all the time, and my friends noticed it.

They said, "He is changing you. You are not the same person anymore, and we miss the fun, bubbly you, and your fabulous laugh."

I knew it, and I still didn't leave him.

One day, I was walking down the street with Sean. He said, "Look at that girl over there."

I said, "Why?"

"Her ass is the kind I like," he replied.

I felt sick. "Why would you say that to me? It makes me feel awful."

"Ah, it's no big deal," he said. "Wise up."

It was a big deal. He enjoyed putting me down, and I could no longer tolerate it.

A few days later, I said, "I am done with this, Sean. You are emotionally abusive, and I deserve better."

He said, "You are off the scale. It's in your DNA. You are the one with the problem." "No, you need help," I said.

"I admit I have anger issues," he said, "but you need to be less sensitive."

"I can't be spoken to like this. I will not accept it," I said.

He said, "Let's have a break."

"OK," I said.

We went our separate ways.

That night, I was devastated. I loved him and missed him, or so I thought. By now I was wired like any partner of an emotionally abusive person and couldn't see any further than the relationship.

We talked things through a few times, but we didn't seem to be getting anywhere.

Eventually, I said, "If you agree to get some help, maybe we can work things out."

He said he was not willing to seek help, but that he was willing to try harder. Then he said, "It will end again anyway, as you will always keep fighting me."

I said, "I have to fight back because I cannot allow you to disrespect me."

This conversation was a sign that we shouldn't get back together, but we did. Of course.

Sometimes I wondered how the fact that we had spent our entire relationship under some form of lockdown or social restrictions had affected us. I thought that we should go on holiday together, to do something fun and normal, form some nice memories together, and get closer to each other. We booked a trip to the west of Ireland, as we could not fly anywhere just yet.

We had so many fights in the days leading up to our vacation that I was wracked with anxiety and didn't even want to go anymore. I forced myself to go on the trip because I still really wanted to make it work. Something about this man made it impossible for me to let him go. Once again, I had found myself in a relationship dynamic that was almost identical to the one I had with my mother.

The vacation started off well. Sean was being lovely, and we enjoyed so many great moments together. There was music, dancing, chatting, and then—*bang*, he was horrible again. He shouted at me in a restaurant, stormed out, and left me sitting there by myself. I was at my lowest. I felt emotionally, mentally, and spiritually drained. I knew I I had to get out of this rollercoaster relationship.

When we returned home, I said I would need some time to think about things. I thought he would to be willing to work on the relationship, but he said he was too old, at fifty-five, to compromise. I had no choice but to walk away. I had to value myself, but it wasn't easy. I had really fallen for him. He was the first man I had loved in eight years, and I had believed he was going to be my future. I guess it just wasn't meant to be.

The New Normal

I spent the next few months feeling really blue. I could not get Sean out of my head. I thought about him as soon as I woke up every morning, and I could not stop talking about him to my friends. They were relieved when I had left him, as they wanted me to be myself again, but they also felt for me as they knew my heart had been broken.

Three weeks after we had broken up, he was back on Tinder. Women were messaging me on Facebook to say he had asked them out. I was devastated. While I couldn't even think about going on a date, he seemed to have moved on completely. This brought back all the heartache I had suffered in the past. I felt rejected all over again, even though I had been the one to walk away. I was so hurt by his ability to discard me and move on almost immediately.

After some time, I recognized that the fact that he didn't take any time to reflect on our relationship might mean that he is the kind of codependent person who needs to always be in a relationship. I remembered what my friend had said about Sean being a narcissist. At the time, I had brushed it off, but now I started to educate myself about narcissistic behavior. As I looked back on our conversations and interactions, I could see that Sean bears all the classic traits of a narcissist. This realization made me sad because he has so many great qualities as well.

At least I knew I had learned some things from my past. I hadn't allowed him to treat me badly. I had stood up for myself and said no. I am so glad I had the strength to get out. I do feel for individuals who aren't able to leave their abusers because they have kids together or for financial reasons. I think many people don't understand how damaging it can be to love a narcissist. It was the first time I had experienced this form of emotional abuse, and it was hard to heal from. I had never met anyone like him before. The time I spent with Sean was one of the biggest lessons of my life.

To keep my mind off Sean, I immersed myself in my work. Things were extremely busy at this stage, as I had landed a few big companies. Still, Sean kept coming into my head. We always dwell on the good times, never the bad.

That November, I traveled to Salt Lake City, Utah, for work. I met with a client I had started doing business with the previous year. We had formed a great working relationship and a lovely friendship, so I was delighted to meet her in person. After I had completed my work commitments, she showed me so many amazing sights. I visited Robert Redford's ski resort, which is gorgeous. I felt like I was in an old Western movie.

Utah is a breathtakingly beautiful state, and I love that Salt Lake City is so close to the mountains. This trip was just what I needed after two years without any international travel, so I savored every second—even the long-haul flight. I appreciated every aspect of travel after having been without it for so long.

Before heading home, I flew out to visit Richard in NYC. I loved spending time with him in his new home, and he brought me to Philadelphia, and Washington, DC. I loved both these cities. Richard had recently broken up with his girlfriend, who he had been seeing for around the same length of time that I had been with Sean. He understood how I was feeling, and he felt that I had made the right decision. Spending some time away in a different country with a different vibe gave me some breathing space. I was able to clear my head and get back on track.

Sean had messaged me while I was in Washington, DC, but I didn't feel a pressing need to respond immediately, considering he had once left me on read for nine days. I decided I would write to him when I knew exactly what I wanted to say to him.

On my way home, during my stopover in Heathrow, I emailed him. I wrote that I had enjoyed some of the times we had spent together, and that I was happy. I wished him well and said I honestly hoped he would find someone who suits him much better than I had.

When I arrived back in Ireland, my friend Pat collected me from the airport, and we went out to dinner so I could tell him all about my adventures. Pat is gentle, quiet, and easygoing. He is a deep and caring person, and we instantly connected as friends as soon as we met.

About a year after I moved to Dublin, he had reached out to me through my blog, and we had chatted for some time before eventually meeting up. After that, we stayed in touch and would meet up about once a month. Each time we met, we would head off into the city with the intention of having a few drinks, but it never quite turned out that way. The night would usually end with us climbing into our respective taxis at some late hour, having had far too much to drink. On those nights out in the city I love, I never wanted to go home. This was long before any of the lockdowns, and the city was always alive.

Pat and I have a great friendship, and over the years he has become a close friend and ally. He truly gets me. On many occasions, I would have been lost without him. I often tell him: *I believe my dad sent you to me.* He reminds me so much of my dad in so many ways.

That Christmas was very difficult for me. For some strange reason, I was missing Sean. More than missing him, I missed having a relationship. I daydreamed about meeting up with him, even if it was just to have a drink together and to wish each other a happy Christmas. Deep down, I knew seeing him would only reopen the wounds and cause me a lot of pain.

Christmas is an emotional time, and when you are lonely it is hard not to idealize the last relationship you had. I kept imagining that if Sean and I hadn't broken up, we would be having a wonderful Christmas together. To bring myself back to reality, I forced myself to remember all the reasons he wasn't right for me: his inability to connect, his lack of empathy, and his unwillingness to compromise. Most importantly, it was the way he made me feel. I reminded myself that I deserve to be with someone who is emotionally available.

To try to get my mind off Sean, I went on a few dates with other guys. I just was not feeling it with anyone, so eventually I decided I would simply enjoy celebrating Christmas with my friends. At that time, things had not yet fully opened up, but we were allowed to go out until ten in the evening, which was better than nothing.

I invited my friends to my home for Christmas Day, as my mum would be spending the day with my brother and his family. I have always loved to entertain and host people in my home, and now I had a big kitchen. It was a great mix of people: Pat; Carol, who I had met soon after moving here; and Patrick, my other friend from Cavan. Patrick is gregarious and entertaining. He loves to recite Oscar Wilde, and he sees himself as Wilde's reincarnation.

Pat helped me out with the cooking, and the four of us enjoyed a wonderful day and evening together. Still, I often thought about Sean. I wondered what he was doing that day and who he was with. Why could I not get this man out of my head? I kept telling myself that in time, it would pass.

Pat had never liked Sean, even though the two of them had never met. Pat knew how much Sean had hurt me. He was proud of me for having had the strength to walk away, and he was glad to see me getting back to my old self.

Pat said, "Why would anyone want to hurt someone with such a beautiful soul?"

I sometimes feel that Pat is the first man in my life who sees me as I am, warts and all.

I have a big heart. It may have been broken many times, but it heals well. I have always had the ability to open it up again in time. I don't hate men; in fact, I love men. I don't hold grudges. The past is the past. I have loved deeply and been deeply loved, so I am more fortunate than many.

Life sometimes sends us a curve ball, but we have the power to decide how to deal with it, and to pick ourselves up and move on. We only get one shot at life, so it's up to us to make it count. There is a big world out there with many people to meet.

As I sit with Zara on the pier in Dún Laoghaire, my happy place, looking out at the Irish Sea, I feel a bright future awaits me here in Dublin. Since moving here four years ago, I have rebuilt my life, survived a pandemic, and made many awesome friends along the way. I have continued to thrive in a tough sales environment and to provide for myself without relying on anyone else.

Reflecting on my losses and acknowledging my strides, I feel empowered, accomplished, and valued. Between leaving the shores of Belfast lough and arriving on the banks of the Liffey, I have loved, lost, and learned a lot. I have found me and come to love myself exactly as I am. And I am still standing.

P.S.

I count myself as having been very fortunate. Even though I have lost a lot, I have also gained a lot, and I am who I am today because of my journey. I am grateful that I have always found the strength to carry on.

At forty-nine, I had reached a point of no return. I believed my life was over, that no one would want me, that no one would employ me, and that I was worthless to society. Unless I made a drastic decision to change my life, I knew I would not be able to keep on going. I was drowning in negativity, self-pity, and self-loathing. I hated who I had become.

I know I am not the only person who has experienced hardship and heartache. It happens to so many of us. While writing this book, I realized how important it is to appreciate what we have and to trust in our own ability to keep moving forward. At my lowest points, I just wanted the pain to go away, and I thought the only way to achieve that was to end my life.

But I didn't really want to leave this earth. I wanted to get my life back. I wanted to keep living and to grow into the person I had always wanted to be. More than anything, I wanted to be me again. I had to dig deep to find my inner strength and the power to rediscover myself.

When I made that brave decision to move to Dublin and make a new start, I had nothing except my belongings, my dog, and my friends. But I knew that starting anew would give me the opportunity to find my inner peace and, ultimately, my happiness. Northern Ireland held nothing for me, except heartache and pain. If I wanted to heal, I would have to move away from what had destroyed me.

It was a big step to leave behind everything I had known and to start again, especially when I had no security. Deep inside, I knew it was the right road for me to take. I was not frightened. I had already lost everything, so I had nothing more to lose. I had to take those first steps towards a life I hoped would bring me the happiness I deserve.

To me, Dublin is a place where I can be free. I came here and decided to start over fresh. I made the conscious decision to always present my authentic self. I soon learned that when you do that, people can sense you are being honest with them, and they are more likely to be honest with you. They are more likely to accept you as you are.

I am blessed to have a lot of people who love me. I have lost some friends along the way, and made new friends, as we all do. Although some friendships may not stand the test of time, I still treasure them, as they were part of my journey. And I am grateful for the friendships that endure.

I am happy to say that my mother and I are in a good place now. I have forgiven her, as I know she didn't know any different and that she loves me. She is in a nursing home, as she has dementia, and I visit her as often as I can. I will always love her. We get only one set of parents, and even though they may not always do the right thing, they are our parents. When they are gone, they are gone.

I miss my dad so much. I would give anything to spend just one day on the beach with him, chatting about everything under the sun. I know he would have been so proud of me for having written this book. I believe he is up there, watching over me and sending me angels to guide me along my journey.

For so many years, I had dreamed of writing a book. Even throughout all the lockdowns, when there were no distractions, I still couldn't get my head together to do it. I believe things happen when the time is right.

In January 2022, I was having lunch with two of my Dublin friends, Jim Quinn and Ann Brehony, who I had met through my blog. They told me: *You have got to start writing your book. We will kick your ass if you don't.*

That was exactly what I needed to hear. I got my laptop out on January 6 and just kept writing until the middle of April. This has been a huge achievement for me. I am proud to share my story of love, loss, and renewed hope.

In writing this book, I discovered the truth about myself. I had never accepted myself as I was. From an early age, I had craved love and acceptance. I had always done whatever I thought I had to do to get other people to accept me. I never felt that little old me could be enough. I thought I had to prove my worth by saying and doing what society expects of me, by having the right material possessions, and by being successful. People usually assume I am Protestant, and I had always let them think that, as I wanted to fit in and be accepted. I worried way too much about what others thought of me and placed too much value on their opinions of me. I allowed too many emotionally unavailable men to take up too much space in my head.

Now I understand that I have always been more than enough, and I no longer care what anyone else thinks of me. It has taken a long time, but instead of needing others to validate me, I have learned to value myself. I am happier and more content than I have ever been and am ready to take on life.

It can take a lifetime to discover who we really are. I spent so much of my life believing I needed a relationship to define me. No-one else can give your life meaning; only you can do that. These days, I am better equipped to find love. I no longer ignore red flags, and I maintain healthy boundaries in my relationships. I remain open-minded and want to keep giving people a chance, as I would like to find my life partner. I now know I am worthy of the right kind of love.

Someday, I will find it.

Acknowledgments

There are many people I would like to thank for their guidance and help in all aspects of my life:

My mother, for her strength. I'm grateful to have inherited this from her. Without it, I may not have been able to endure so much loss in my life.

My brother, Barry, and my sister, Brenda, for everything we shared. We once were very close, and although we have grown apart over the years, you are my family. I love you, and I always will.

Aunt Pat, for always having understood and supported me.

My friends from Northern Ireland, for standing by my side and seeing me through my darkest days.

My friends in Dublin, for including me in their world and making me feel like I have been part of it for many years.

The friends who are no longer traveling with me on my journey, for helping me to grow.

My customers, for believing in me and working with me over the years.

Readers of my blog, for their friendship and support from across the miles. Being able to connect with them has meant so much to me.

About the Author

Denise Robinson was born in Belfast at the start of the Troubles and moved to the countryside to escape the conflict. At eighteen she moved back to Belfast, where she lived until moving to Dublin at the age of forty-nine.

After leaving school, Robinson entered the printing industry. She went on to establish her own print brokerage, which she ran for eleven years while also modeling with a local agency and working at motor shows.

Robinson still works in print. In recent years, she has become an inspirational blogger. She lives in Dún Laoghaire with her little cocker spaniel, Zara.

Printed in Great Britain
by Amazon